THE COMEBACK BLUEPRINT

The Comeback Blueprint

Winning at Life After Addiction

Katherine Straughn

©2026 All Rights Reserved. No portion of this book may be reproduced, stored in a retrieval system, or transmitted in any form or by any means—electronic, mechanical, photocopy, recording, scanning, or other—except for brief quotations in critical reviews or articles without the prior permission of the author.

Published by Game Changer Publishing

Paperback ISBN: 979-8-90158-500-9

Hardcover ISBN: 979-8-90158-023-3

Digital ISBN: 979-8-90158-026-4

www.GameChangerPublishing.com

*To my family, the Queens, and the ones who loved me back to life.
Thank you for giving me the courage to speak the truth I once hid.
Your faith in me helped me find mine, and this book
is proof that we really do recover.*

READ THIS FIRST

To everyone who picked up *The Comeback Blueprint*, thank you.

Your support means more than words can express. Every page of this book was written with the hope that someone, somewhere, would find the courage to believe that it's never too late to rebuild.

If my story has reminded you that God still has a plan for your life, then every tear, prayer, and late-night writing session was worth it. From the bottom of my heart, thank you for walking this journey with me. I would like to connect!

Scan the QR Code Here:

THE COMEBACK BLUEPRINT

WINNING AT LIFE
AFTER ADDICTION

KATHERINE STRAUGHN

CONTENTS

Introduction	ix
1. The Performance Trap	1
2. The Wake-Up Call	11
3. The Cost of Not Quitting	23
4. Geographics and External Façades	33
5. California Dreamin'	43
6. The Gift of an Eskimo	51
7. From Survival to Calling	61
8. From Pain to Purpose	73
9. Healed by Horses, Humbled by Dogs	85
10. The Rise of SoberKatt: Owning My Story Out Loud	93
11. The Queens Call	97
12. Discipline, Alignment & the Gym That Changed Everything	103
Conclusion	109

INTRODUCTION

I didn't always believe that change was possible. For years, I struggled, repeating patterns and breaking resolutions that "today was going to be different," only to slip back into the exact behavior I'd sworn off the night before. Addiction convinced me I was broken beyond repair.

But God met me, not in the waters of baptism, not at church, not even when I deserved a second chance. He met me at my lowest and pulled me out of the pits. I promised to help set others free if He would break my chains, and that is exactly why I wrote this book.

This is a story about my life: the chaos, the pain, and the journey of rebuilding. My hope is that when someone finishes reading it, they realize that if God can do this for me, He can do it for you.

INTRODUCTION

My story is not just a book but a roadmap for anyone who has struggled with the shame of their past, the grips of addiction, or the lies that come with not stepping into their purpose. This book is for anyone who wants a new future but doesn't know where to begin.

Here you'll find honesty. I'm not going to sugarcoat the process. It is hard, but it is so worth it. You will find courage and hope. This is not about perfection; it's about progress and *purpose*. I'm going to ask you to step out and choose freedom over bondage, faith over fear, and *action* over excuses.

I wrote this book for the woman who feels she's gone too far and can't come back. To the man who believes he has wasted too many years going in the wrong direction, so he thinks, *What's the point?* I wrote this for you.

You're not too far gone! The chains you carry are only part of your story, just the beginning. And when you're finally free, you'll inspire others to do the same.

How to use this book: This book isn't only for reading; it's for recognizing and breaking patterns in your life that may be holding you back. More importantly, this is a guide you can use to step into your God-given purpose. Maybe your story doesn't mirror mine, and maybe addiction is not part of your story, but we all have something that holds us back. Maybe it's a mindset, a fear, a relationship. My goal is that this book helps you identify areas of your life or patterns of past/current behavior that are keeping you from your highest self and, ultimately, serving others.

At the end of every chapter, there will be space for self-reflection, which is designed to help you do the work necessary for true transformation. This book will give you an opportunity to own it and then do something about it (act on it).

SET YOUR INTENTION FOR THIS BOOK

This isn't just a story; it's a process. Before you turn the page, decide what you want to get out of it.

Is it healing? Purpose? Peace? Courage?

Write your intention on the first page and keep it as your north star throughout the book.

Transformation doesn't happen in theory; it happens in practice. Promise yourself that you'll complete every Own it and Act on it section honestly, even when it feels uncomfortable.

Own it: Take a quiet moment to be present with where you are right now. Don't worry, because even if you are struggling, you don't need to have all the answers right now.

Ask yourself: *What part of my life feels out of alignment with who God created me to be?* Write down whatever comes up.

Face it: This is where you stop running from the truth and turn toward it with courage. What you refuse to face will continue to run your life. What you're willing to face, God can finally heal.

Ask yourself: *What have I been avoiding, denying, or minimizing… and what is it costing me?* Write down the reality you've been scared to look at. Not to shame yourself but to **free** yourself.

Clarity is not punishment.
Clarity is freedom.

Act on it: This is where we will look at the roots of your patterns and beliefs. Before something can be healed, it must be revealed.

ONE
THE PERFORMANCE TRAP

This is a story of how I nearly ruined my life and how God gave me a second chance. Hitting rock bottom gave me the place to create something real at last. Out of the ashes and broken pieces of the life I thought I wanted, I began creating a legacy, one that led others to also believe in their redemption.

I squandered hundreds of thousands of dollars in lost opportunities, relationships, and battles fought in silence. I've clawed my way back to the surface after having rebuilt again and again. I've lived two lives: one the world saw in the light of day, and the other one no one noticed when the lights went out (and there was nothing worth seeing).

But before the addiction, the broken ties, the bottles, the powders, the potions, there was a little girl, barefoot in the fields of Aurora, Colorado, digging in the dirt and chasing anything that moved. Snakes and lizards were her first choice, but the neighbor's cat or dog would do. With sun-kissed skin, curly white-blonde hair, no shoes, a red bandana around her neck, and a fearless spirit with a defiant streak, she earned the nickname "Sass."

I wasn't born rich or privileged. Both my parents worked hard and let me know that earning a fair share of society's wealth was worth it. They loved me unconditionally, giving me everything I could need as a child. But even in an environment filled with love, I felt an unexplainable sadness. A conflict within myself that left a privileged, adored little girl feeling alienated, invisible, and out of place.

My parents were college graduates whose military parents had instilled discipline, loyalty, and grit. My mom had my brother at 30 and me, four years later. I was born in Denver, Colorado, healthy, loved, and safe. And yet, ever since I can remember, I carried this kind of quiet ache. The fact is, even as a little girl, I often felt like I didn't belong, like I had been switched at birth and somehow arrived in the wrong place.

I always had such a hard time with other kids my age. I was acutely sensitive, aware of feelings that most children could not name, and I found my sanctuary in animals. A rabbit named "Cloudy" was one of my first pets. My mother and I spotted him at a garage sale, and although I'm not sure he was actually for sale, we somehow persuaded the owners to let us buy him for five dollars.

Cloudy was the meanest rabbit I ever had, unfortunately. I had fantasized about holding him, curling up with him, and maybe even sleeping beside him, but he fought back and would bite and didn't want anything to do with me. Eventually, my parents swapped him out for a hamster, and soon our home was filled with critters: snakes, lizards, and whatever I could locate in the yard.

My parents always fostered my fondness for animals, even if it meant coming home to what looked like a backyard zoo. I didn't wear shoes until age seven, and my hair was long, ruffled, and white-blonde. My mom even paid my babysitter to brush it because I wouldn't allow anyone else to go near it. My nickname "Sass" made me feel like I owned the neighborhood.

When I was about eight years old, my mom and dad got me a little red Barbie Corvette, and I would cruise down the street and park in other people's driveways. Often, I would sneak in and steal snacks or even one of my neighbors' pets and take them back home to my room. A knock at the door would usually be followed by the question, "Is Sass here?" as a nervous neighbor looked for a missing cat or dog. My parents never bought me a cat or a dog, but that didn't stop me from adopting half the block.

That independence, the audacity to break out and claim my space, carried on into adulthood. When my parents threw parties, I would take a sip from the drinks when no one was looking. They weren't heavy drinkers, but their friends were, and it all seemed so fun, so carefree. I didn't feel the full effects of alcohol until I was thirteen or so. I was at a friend's house for the weekend. We lied to our parents, saying we were having a sleepover, and her older brother had packed red Solo cups full of beer for us. When the other girls took small sips and wrinkled their noses in disgust, something different happened to me: I loved it.

I felt an overwhelming sense of excitement, like I couldn't get alcohol into my body fast enough. When I started to feel its effects, it was as if someone had put an oxygen mask over me, transforming my black-and-white world into vibrant color. It was just like what I've read in Alcoholics Anonymous literature; I felt like I had finally "arrived." Suddenly, I was no longer lonely, awkward in my own skin, or afraid to talk to people. With that liquid courage, I became funny, pretty, and smart. I found myself engaging easily with others.

The next morning, as the alcohol wore off, the girls I was with expressed their resolve never to drink again, saying it had been too much. But I felt differently. I thought, *Why would I want to stop?* That night was incredible, and I never wanted to feel anything less than that exhilaration again. I even looked for alcohol around the house, convinced that this newfound sensation would be my new survival mechanism.

My whole life up until that night was full of restlessness, irritability, and discontent. I was too alienated in my own skin and lacked confidence, but drinking brought a sense of ease, belonging, and relief. I would drink at home, at friends' houses, anywhere I could. A year or two later, marijuana came into the picture, and with it came that same sensation of connectedness, a false calm.

Life became a crossroads once I graduated from middle school and entered high school. My brother went away to college, and the house suddenly felt empty, heavy, and quiet. Left alone with my thoughts, I turned to new highs to fill the void. I was on the varsity cheer team as a freshman, and for the first time, I felt like I fit in. But in time, I began experiencing imposter syndrome. When I was elected captain, I thought, *If they really knew me, they wouldn't have picked me.*

I immersed myself in activities: Future Business Leaders of America, advanced placement courses, and anything that would make me look "put together." On the outside, I was thriving. But on the inside, I was running from the truth. I became an expert in fitting in. I could shift and adapt like a chameleon, becoming an athlete, a student, a leader, whatever people needed me to be. The more roles I fulfilled, the less the world saw the real me. It was a tactic that worked, at least for a time.

The only time I felt at ease, like I could finally exhale, was when I was drinking. Alcohol became my shortcut to belonging, a way to quiet the noise in my head and slip into a version of myself that didn't feel like an act. I started going to parties at other schools, living a double life: the responsible, hardworking cheerleader with good grades by day and the reckless girl chasing escape by night.

This pattern carried through my high school years. I bounced from one group to another, my behavior growing bolder each time. Though I never touched hard drugs, I would "drink and drive," convincing myself I was in control when in reality, I was anything but. My parents didn't know what to do. They took my car away, grounded me, and pleaded with me to stop. My mom would look at me with worry and ask, "Don't you think you have a future? Aren't you afraid of what will happen if you get caught? Have you thought about how this could affect your life, your college, your dreams?" At the time, I brushed her off. I couldn't see past the moment. I wasn't thinking about the future; I was just trying to survive the present.

Imposter syndrome is that deep, nagging feeling that you don't belong, that you have somehow fooled people into thinking you are more capable, talented, or deserving than you actually are. I didn't mind; I was rebellious, and I liked being the child they couldn't control. That was part of the essence of who I was.

Even at a young age, I felt everything deeply. My emotions were overwhelming. At fourteen, I remember those emotional outbursts, as if I had come into the world like a raw nerve, ten times stronger than everyone around me.

My dad used to comment on my sensitivity, but I don't think anyone understood the fullness of what that actually meant. I needed to express how I felt, to be seen, heard, and understood. But my parents came from military backgrounds where emotions were repressed, and being strong meant being composed. They cherished me deeply but did not always have the resources to handle the emotional intensity I carried. So it is no surprise that I turned to drinking and drugs for an outlet. I am not blaming my parents. No one knew how I could manage the weight of my feelings, not even me. We were all doing the best we could with what we knew.

What began as curiosity with drinking turned into a coping mechanism. It was frightening, I was conflicted, and I struggled to get through the days, waking up worried about what would happen to me if my coach or the teachers found out what I was doing. I felt this enormous pressure to hold a public image. If I could convince everyone else I was okay on the outside, maybe I could convince myself that I was okay on the inside, too. So I did everything I could to maintain that image, smiling, achieving, leading, all while trying to quiet the voice in my head telling me I wasn't enough. I fretted that my friendships were also conditional and that my varsity captain gig was brief, because if anyone got to really see who I was underneath it, everything would come crashing down.

Eventually, I reached a point where I thought, *If they're going to strip me of these things anyway, and if I'm not the person they believe me to be, I might as well start acting like the person I wanted to be, the rebellious wild child.* Then I would feel guilt and remorse and vow to do better that day.

However, I could never let anyone get close enough. It became a good defense mechanism to keep people at arm's length. I could be the jock in the weight room, take all the AP classes, compete in debate meets on weekends, attend Future Business Leaders of

America retreats, and cheerlead. I compartmentalized all these aspects of my life so I could act however I wanted to.

I maintained whatever image those around me needed me to have, but deep down, I knew that if they truly found out who I was, they wouldn't like me because I didn't like myself. I had no idea how to be okay in my own skin.

I became a chameleon, skilled at telling people what they wanted to hear while doing whatever I needed to behind closed doors to self-soothe and feel at ease.

All of this worked until I turned eighteen during my senior year, when I was finally called out.

Self-Reflection: Maybe you didn't grow up exactly the way I did, and your version of "high expectations" looks different or comes from a different place than mine. Regardless of *where* it comes from, the pressure to perform to earn love can feel lonely and lead to deep wounds. This is your space to start exploring that.

Theme: Identity rooted in performance, not authenticity, or the duality between external image and internal reality.

Own it: Have I ever felt I could only be accepted for "what I've done" vs. "who I am"?

Face it: What messages did I receive about achievement and success? Did I ever learn that I'm only valuable when I'm producing, performing, or achieving?

Sit with this. Be honest. Name the wound, so it stops running your life.

Act on it: What's one label or expectation I can release today? What would it look like to choose authenticity over performance?

TWO
THE WAKE-UP CALL

When I was eighteen, I was trying to find my way.

I felt a bit nervous as I was looking at colleges and applying. No one had discovered all the drinking I'd been doing, but my mom had reached a point where she didn't know what to do with me. She asked, "How do you think you're going to get into college acting this way?"

I told her, "I'll figure it out."

One of the notable traits of addicts is our "I'll figure it out" attitude. I was working, which was another thing my family instilled in me. Although I never wanted for anything, they taught me the value of hard work and earning a dollar. If I wanted something, I had to work for it.

I started working at a restaurant as a hostess when I was sixteen and eventually became a server. I worked at a steakhouse in Centennial, Colorado, and I loved it. It was such a fun job! I enjoyed wearing a cowboy hat, boots, and jeans, cultivating an alter ego.

I was great at having alter egos and living double lives, so this felt very natural. I would be working and bragging about the upperclassmen I was drinking with, the drugs I was using, and the keg parties I was attending. There was one man, another server at the restaurant, whom I had a major crush on, but he was never impressed by my antics. In fact, he seemed disinterested in getting to know me as a friend. I could tell he even disliked me.

One day, I worked up the courage to ask him why he wasn't interested in me. I had a shameless crush on him and wasn't accustomed to being told no. I thought maybe he didn't like women, so I pulled him aside and asked, "Are you gay? Why aren't you into me?"

He replied plainly that I wasn't a Christian and that, frankly, he was disgusted by my behavior. I was stunned, not only because no one had ever said that to me before but also because he had called me out for the first time in my life. He had seen through my façade, and it was the first time I hadn't been able to blend in.

Later that night, while we were rolling silverware in the back, I sat next to him and asked, "What did you mean by that?" He shared the gospel of Jesus with me. He explained that all the struggles and validations I sought for acceptance, things I believed I needed to earn, had already been given to me by God. He said that I was created perfectly and that God loves me just as I am. He emphasized that I didn't have to strive for acceptance from people. "Living a life with Jesus takes all that away," he said. "He died on the cross for your sins and loves you. You don't need to do anything except follow Him and accept Him into your heart."

For the first time, it felt like I truly heard "the Message." I had attended church services before where the gospel of Jesus was shared, but this time was different. It was as if *"the scales had fallen from my eyes."* Suddenly, the words I'd heard so many times before came alive, and I could finally "see" and understand their true meaning (Acts 9:18).

That night, I went home and headed to our guest bedroom, where I knew there was an old Bible. I opened it and began reading John 3:16, along with some verses from Matthew that I had been given by my server friend at the restaurant. I got on my knees, and even though the old English in that Bible was challenging for me to understand, in that moment, I felt a profound transformation in my heart that night. I asked Jesus into my heart. I sensed something shift within me.

When I returned to work, I shared what had happened my coworker, and he invited me to church with him. I didn't know it at the time, but he was essentially the son of a preacher. We began attending church together, and I started attending their high school and college Bible study.

There was a major shift in my behavior and my heart. For the first time, I felt like I belonged. It was a different feeling from when I was younger, drinking at thirteen and getting high; this was peace, a peace that surpassed all understanding. I didn't fully grasp it, but I knew I loved it and wanted more. So, I dove in wholeheartedly, attending church and Bible study… and began dating the man from the restaurant.

My family noticed a significant change in my behavior and was excited about the new person I had become. They loved their new daughter, even though they were a bit wary, unsure if this change would last. They weren't anti-religious, but faith wasn't a part of their lives. His family, on the other hand, was incredibly loving. He had one brother and two sisters, who enveloped me with love and understanding. They would have family meals and discuss things that we never talked about in my family. I craved that connection and started to feel like I was a part of something special.

Shortly after we started dating on my 19th birthday, he proposed to me. My parents reluctantly agreed to the engagement because they appreciated the change in me and thought he was a great man. They had never seen me so happy. Their only condition was that I had to graduate. They felt I should finish my education and asked that we wait until I graduated before getting married. However, he and I felt differently, that we could get married and I would continue my education afterward.

After about a year of engagement, when I was twenty, I told my parents we were done waiting to get married. We were eager to start our life together, committed to remaining pure before marriage. We both felt ready.

At that time, we were actively involved in the church, believing it was the right path for us. We participated in premarital counseling and did everything "by the book." I even got baptized. While attending school in Boulder, Colorado, I felt isolated, especially because I was at a large party school.

I was now a very devout Christian who had transformed my entire life. I shifted from partying, drinking, and casual relationships, behaviors that were considered unacceptable in the university setting, to becoming a committed, devout Christian woman who was engaged to a preacher's son. It was striking to think about the dichotomy between my past life and my current one.

Walking around campus was challenging. I often felt out of place and experienced feelings of inadequacy and isolation, which all came flooding back. Unless I was with my fiancé (he attended a different school in Denver), I found it hard to relate to others. I spent a lot of time driving and didn't enjoy the typical college experience. While I was living in the dorms, I often longed to see him or attend church together.

I found a church near my school to attend, but I still struggled to feel a sense of belonging. My heart transformation was sincere, but there's something to be said for being part of a community of like-minded individuals. Although there were many Christians at college, it was all new territory for me. As a "baby" Christian, I was still learning about my faith, and even though I was joining Bible studies and seeking out Christian relationships, I often felt disconnected. Those familiar feelings of isolation, being an outsider, and feeling uncomfortable in my own skin returned. This was not at all what I had imagined my college experience would be.

During college, I had a few slip-ups that took me back to my old life, primarily because I was trying to fit in with others. A couple of times, I ended up getting completely drunk, but it didn't happen often, and each time I woke up feeling remorseful. I was dedicated to my fiancé and our new life.

To cope with the feelings of inadequacy, I began channeling my energy into running, something I now recognize might have been a precursor to alcoholism. I started running a lot, often covering twenty miles a day and averaging twelve miles regularly. Being in college gave me the time to do this. I also worked at a brewery, ironically, but I didn't struggle with drinking there.

As for my education, I took it seriously because I had to pay for it myself with student loans. My parents weren't covering my tuition, which made me respect my college experience a little more. I noticed that many students at my school came from wealthy backgrounds and didn't seem to care about their studies. They often drove expensive cars and had access to unlimited trust funds, taking their education for granted. In contrast, I felt a strong responsibility toward my studies since the financial burden was mine to bear. I worked hard, ran a lot, and was very fit at twenty years old.

On June 11, 2004, we got married, and although we had alcohol at our wedding, I only took a sip of champagne. We had a fairly large wedding in Centennial, Colorado, organized by my amazing family, who threw us a fantastic celebration. They had concerns about my young age, but they recognized my dedication to working hard and excelling in school. While they saw my consistency, they were unaware of the imposter syndrome that was creeping in.

After marrying my fiancé (I'll call him "John"), we got involved in a church in Broomfield, Colorado, and participated in youth ministry. We took the kids backpacking and helped with summer camps, which made for a fantastic first few years of marriage. I also became extremely into fitness and running; I began by completing half-marathons and eventually worked my way up to full marathons.

A significant part of my story is my sweet dog Bella. I finally got a dog in my sophomore year of college when I was eighteen. I lived in the dorms my freshman year, but during my second year, I moved in with two other girls who were Christians. My parents put some money in my bank account for groceries, but I ended up spending it to get Bella. I wasn't even allowed to have a dog in my apartment at that time, but I couldn't resist. All I had ever wanted was a dog.

"Bella" was an adorable, three-pound Jack Russell, and she became my companion throughout those lonely college years. I would take her to class with me, and she really helped me get through that tough time.

I still found comfort in Bella's companionship when John and I would hike the Flatirons every day together. She was such a cool dog. However, I started running so much in college that Bella would actually hide when I grabbed her leash; she seemed over it! Jack Russells have a lot of energy, so it was surprising that she didn't want to join me anymore.

In true dog-lover fashion, I decided to get another dog. His name was Jackson, and he was a mix between a Pitbull and a Labrador. Jackson was full of energy when I adopted him from the Boulder Humane Society. He couldn't wait to leave the cage, and his long legs made him look like he was an incredible runner. However, after bringing him home, he barely moved.

I called the vet, convinced there was something wrong, like I had received a "lemon." The doctor advised me to bring him in for testing, and they conducted blood work and other tests. The vet discovered that Jackson was perfectly fine; his heart just beat slowly. He wasn't sick; he was simply a laid-back dog who preferred to chill and be by my side at home rather than go for runs. So, I ended up with two dogs who became my best friends in college.

I spent a lot of time outdoors again, much like I had in childhood, hiking and enjoying nature. As my husband was both working and attending school full-time during my remaining years of college, I often felt isolated and alone. However, I found solace in my animals, taking them everywhere with me, telling myself that if I could just stay the course, everything would improve once I graduated. I believed I would "find happiness on the other side" (a familiar feeling for me).

We would often have his family over for dinner, and I became incredibly domesticated. I created weekly menus, did the shopping and budgeting, packed his lunches, and cooked dinner. I remember hosting his family at our little condo in Westminster, Colorado. They would bring a bottle of wine, and I would have just one glass. But after that, my mind would become completely consumed with thoughts about whether someone would finish their glass of wine or, if I took the dishes to the sink, they would think it was strange if they found out I finished their wine. Other times, I found myself wondering why they weren't drinking more or thinking about whether I could go and get another bottle to hide for my future supply.

It became so frustrating to me when I realized I could not drink the way I wanted. At the time, I didn't understand that this was a manifestation of my mental obsession and the allergy that triggered once I began drinking. I just thought it was an annoyance.

So, I decided to stop drinking entirely. When I went out, I'd think, *Why have one drink? If I can't drink the way I want to, which is to get completely obliterated, I'll just have none.* I believed I was doing remarkably well because I was abstaining from alcohol. I was running regularly, going to school, and participating actively in my church and youth group.

I graduated from college in 2008. Learning that I was already "chosen" without having to earn or perform flipped the script for me. However, feelings of imposter syndrome crept back in. I spent some time walking in freedom, but it didn't take long for those old voices to creep back in: the fear that I was just pretending, that if people saw me for who I really was (even Jesus), they'd know I wasn't who I said I was. I thought, *This isn't really me. This won't last. If John finds out who I really am, he will leave me. This isn't where I truly belong.*

The spiritual drift no one talks about is accepting Jesus into your life while still feeling like you have something to prove. Maybe it's not Jesus for you. Maybe you've experienced freedom in an area of your life, but you act like you're still in chains. Let's pause here and get honest:

Own it: What parts of my life are built on image, not integrity? Am I still trying to earn something I've been given?

Face it: Where have I drifted from my core identity for the approval of others? What is one thing people would be surprised to know I've secretly been struggling with?

Act on it: What's *one* truth about my identity that I need to take back today? What's one mask I can put down, and what would that look like?

Invitation to accept Jesus: If what you read in this chapter stirred something in you to know Jesus personally, you don't have to wait. He is ready to meet you!

A prayer to accept Jesus:

Lord Jesus,

I know that I am a sinner, and I ask for your forgiveness. I believe You died on the cross for my sins and rose from the dead.

Today, I turn from my old ways, and I invite You into my heart and life. I want to trust and follow You as my Lord and Savior. Thank you for loving me and making me new. Amen.

Scan the QR code to have a free Bible sent to you!

THREE
THE COST OF NOT QUITTING

I graduated with a bachelor's degree in Business Administration with an emphasis in Marketing. There hadn't been a dedicated sales program in colleges at that time, as there is now, so I joined a sales bootcamp in downtown Boulder, a rigorous, boiler-room-style program that simulated real-world cold calling. It was a free bootcamp, but it cost us everything.

About 30 or 40 of us started together, beginning our days at 6 a.m. and often staying until 10 p.m. I did well in that sort of environment because the pressure was unrelenting. I have always known how to push through difficult times and perform under pressure. By the end, I was among the top program graduates and started pairing up with companies looking for young professionals with some sales exposure. Corporate sales roles then were scarce and competitive, so landing an opportunity felt like acknowledgment, a confirmation that all my hard work and effort had paid off.

I signed up for a job with an Indian call center as a regional sales representative soon after the bootcamp. I was young, I was inexperienced, and out of my element in many ways, but I was hungry and committed, and I was confident I could make a sale. For a while, I wasn't drinking. I had a few slips, a night of drinking too much here and there, but nothing I couldn't rationalize or conceal behind my work ethic.

That all changed when I went to my first sales conference in Houston. The atmosphere was electric: open bars, late-night networking, endless toasts to success. I hadn't told anybody that I stopped drinking; yet when my colleagues ordered cocktails, I didn't want to feel isolated. So I joined them. And just like that, I picked up right where I left off after high school.

If you've ever attended corporate conferences, you know they can be a bit like spring break for adults, where the challenge is to enjoy as much drinking and debauchery as possible without getting caught and while keeping your job. In those initial conferences, I didn't face any real consequences. I had fun, got drunk, and felt part of the sales team. They enjoyed my company; I was the life of the party, loud and entertaining. I thought, *I can do this!*

I chose not to tell my husband about my experiences, slipping back into that double life: questioning whether he really needed to know and if it was truly a big deal. After all, nothing noteworthy happened; we just had sales meetings and drinks. Gradually, I began to request more travel opportunities.

I was attending numerous conferences and having client dinners, and over time, alcohol became more prevalent in my life. What I didn't realize was that I had ignited an allergy to alcohol. They say that during periods of sobriety, alcoholism is doing push-ups in the parking lot, waiting for you, but that was not the case for me. My alcoholism was progressive and fatal; it wanted me dead, but it would settle for me being drunk.

What happened was that I had an insatiable appetite for alcohol. I thought that by giving in to these urges, I'd be satisfied, but that was never true. In fact, the more I gave in, the stronger those urges became. I started drinking at home, hiding bottles, and suggesting things to myself like, *Why don't we have a bottle of wine with dinner?*

My husband would respond, "What? No, that's crazy." I would try to sneak around it at home. Eventually, he sent me to an AA meeting. I remember we had just moved to a home in Broomfield, and the AA meeting was within walking distance. I walked there but didn't actually go into the meeting room. I thought, *This is so stupid. What am I doing here? I don't have a problem. I just didn't get to drink like I wanted to in college.*

I convinced myself that I was just "sowing my wild oats" and having fun like everyone else. Why could everyone else have fun, but I couldn't? I felt annoyed that John didn't like the person I was, and I began to experience a stark division between my life as a heavy drinker and the fun party girl who felt alive and authentic. I felt I had to hide that side of myself from him because he wouldn't allow it. I kept telling myself I wasn't harming anyone.

While attending a sales conference, I felt self-righteous about my drinking; it seemed okay to me because I wasn't hurting anyone. Things seemed to be going well. I was making good money, I felt part of my company, and my marriage was decent, considering I was living a double life.

As time went on, the consequences of my drinking started to escalate. Believing that the job was the problem, I began to think that quitting was the solution. I never considered that alcohol itself could be the issue or that my behavior, especially my dishonesty with my husband about the amount I was drinking, might be at fault. I never entertained the idea that if I stopped drinking, maybe the other consequences would cease as well. I thought I just needed to "do better next time." If only I had eaten more before drinking or avoided certain places.

At this time, I was around twenty-two years old. I was young, though that's not an excuse. I was facing alcoholism, which I believe is a fatal, progressive disease, yet I treated it as though I just needed to "sow my wild oats." We sought counseling, and the counselor suggested that I find a new job and stop drinking. I agreed to those suggestions, but when it came to my marriage, I wasn't planning to stay.

John took a great job opportunity, so we rented out our house and moved to the mountains of Colorado. We relocated to a small mountain town, and I had no idea that this would become my biggest downfall. Shortly after the move, I took over an insurance agency. We began attending a new church and made friends with a different crowd. We changed our entire lives.

I became the owner of the insurance agency very quickly and got licensed for property, health, casualty, and commercial auto within just two months. Our entire lives transformed because that was my "modus operandi." I believed that if I could change the outside, I could change the inside, too.

For a few months, everything seemed pretty good. We were active in our new church and participated in mountain bike racing and skiing. We embraced this wonderful, active lifestyle with other like-minded couples. However, it wasn't long before a client came in and threw a bag of cocaine on my desk. I ended up doing it with her, which reignited the guilt and shame I'd been carrying. My insatiable appetite quickly flared back to life, and soon after, I started drinking again.

I remember going to church with John and our friends, observing how they worshiped God, and feeling like I didn't belong there. I thought I would rather be drunk and high, and I questioned whether I was truly saved. I wondered if my relationship with God, my baptism, and the heart transformation I had claimed were real, because I felt more alive when I was under the influence.

I repeated all these thoughts to myself over and over again. It was such hell, and he didn't want to divorce me. He was an incredible man of faith, always willing to come find me, no matter the horrible circumstances. I once ran away to Mexico, and everything fell apart. It didn't go well. In that moment, I was desperate to change, wanting to run back to church, become whole again, and feel clean and grounded for the first time in years.

But it was only a matter of time before my resolve met something I didn't understand back then, which I now know was active alcoholism. Alcoholism is confusing because it isn't caused by alcohol; it's treated with alcohol. If I hadn't treated my alcoholism with alcohol, I would have turned to a man, drugs, or other experiences to cope.

I thought that once I experienced life, things like drinking, drugs, and relationships, I'd be able to "settle down" and become a mature adult afterward. I could look back and say I had a fun time in my life, even if it was in my twenties instead of college.

I genuinely believed that marrying young was my mistake and that I needed to end things with John to get everything out of my system. I also felt like I had married too young and wanted to make up for lost time by partying, and I didn't want to continue to hurt him because I truly loved him. He didn't deserve any of this. Hurt people hurt people, and I just kept piling on the guilt and shame. I felt terrible and had no idea how to stop coping with alcohol.

Reluctantly, John granted me a divorce and expressed hope for better things for me. Afterward, I moved in with a mutual friend I was using cocaine with, and she also happened to be a severe alcoholic. That's when things really started to spiral out of control for me.

Self-Reflection: Delaying the decision to confront addiction and being caught up in a life of lies made my entire life unravel. The cost was cumulative over time, not all at once. Bit by bit, I lost myself and those closest to me. What was more confusing was the internal erosion of self-worth, the burden of guilt and shame, while on the outside (in my career and relationships), I appeared functional.

The cost of not quitting is rarely a single DUI or loss of a job, but something far deeper. The cost is the unraveling of self, the look in the eyes of loved ones who don't know how to help you anymore, the guilt and the shame that follow you like a dark cloud.

Thankfully, this isn't where the story ends; forgiveness and healing can be restored by grace. You don't have to fix yourself before coming to God. You just have to come.

Own it: What in my life have I convinced myself is "normal" that is actually hurting others? What are the lies or half-truths that I've been telling myself?

Face it: What truth have I been running from that God is gently calling me to face today?

Act on it: What is one small but honest thing I can do today to align my actions with God's truth instead of my old patterns?

Who do I need to apologize to, set a boundary with, or tell the truth to?

What would obedience look like in the next 24 hours?

PRACTICAL APPLICATION: ACT TO TRANSFORM

Use A.C.T. as a call to action to move from reflection into real transformation:

Acknowledge

- Identify the pattern or behavior that's no longer serving you.
- Be honest. Name it without sugarcoating or minimizing it.

Example: "I acknowledge that I use alcohol to avoid discomfort and maintain a false sense of control."

Confess (To Yourself and One Safe Person)

- Honesty breaks the shame cycle. Whether in a journal, a trusted friend, a therapist, or a spiritual mentor, say it out loud.

Example: "I've been living a double life, and I need help finding my way back to wholeness."

Take One Step

- Not the whole journey. Just the next *right* step.
    - Schedule a therapy appointment.
    - Go to one AA/NA/Al-Anon meeting.
    - Tell your partner one truth.
    - Pour out the alcohol.
    - Turn off the noise and sit with yourself.

Action is the antidote to despair. Small steps compound over time.

This chapter isn't just a confession; it's an invitation. To tell the truth. To stop negotiating with self-destruction. To see that **the cost of not quitting is a slow erosion of your truest self**. But transformation doesn't begin with perfection; it begins with one act of courage.

FOUR
GEOGRAPHICS AND EXTERNAL FAÇADES

I was so confused as to why God felt distant. I believed I had done everything I needed to in order to overcome my struggles: I'd become a Christian, been baptized, and entered into a marriage that honored God. But now that I was officially single, I felt overwhelmed by guilt and shame for ruining my marriage. I had no guardrails left and found myself in full-blown rebellion against God. I had nothing holding me back.

I still owned the insurance company, but running it under the strain of having my addiction in full-blown chaos was exhausting. The pressure of holding everything together in my business, my image, my unraveling personal life was crushing. Cocaine had become a regular part of my routine, and around that time, I was introduced to the prescription Adderall. I convinced my therapist that I was simply overwhelmed from the divorce and the stress of running a company, and that I just needed help focusing. In reality, I was feeding the same disease that was quietly destroying everything I had built.

I was still in the mountains, surrounded by affluent people who had easy access to drugs and alcohol. We partied a lot, and I tried to work as little as possible. At that time, I still had my two dogs.

About six months into this partying lifestyle, drinking every night, closing my shop early, and not opening it on weekends, I realized that I couldn't manage a successful business alongside my addiction. Consequently, I sold the business back to the company and moved back to Denver.

At that point, I didn't have a job and lacked career opportunities. However, my brother had a home there that he only occupied part-time, as he traveled for work between Denver and California. He offered me a place to stay in exchange for helping look after his dog and managing the house.

I took a job with a company that was 100 percent commission-based. I loved it, but I struggled to manage life and work alongside my addiction, and ultimately, it didn't work out. I needed something more stable and began searching for other opportunities. Eventually, I found a position at NetSuite, a software company. They were initially reluctant to hire me because I didn't have a technical background, but they recognized my experience as a business owner, my degree, and my sales background, so they gave me a chance.

I ended up working at this amazing company that was launching great products, and we were closing deals consistently. I became one of their top sales representatives. At this time, I was still partying, but the structured environment of going into an office provided a bit more supervision and support.

For the first time in a while, I felt a sense of fulfillment in my job, like I was finally accomplishing something meaningful. We were extremely busy, and the work helped distract me from my sadness and depression over my lost marriage, as well as the guilt and shame from previous years. I was truly enjoying the work environment.

I figured out a way to help clients buy my product and provide them with an incredible website that enhanced the success of their companies. I introduced them to partners in the industry for fulfillment, drop shipping, and various other aspects that contribute to their growth. One of my gifts is being a connector, so it was rewarding to work with clients who had a budget. I sold them outstanding products and connected them to an ecosystem of other professionals who could assist in their success. I truly enjoyed the work.

During that time, I became one of the top sales representatives and was making good money. When I was living in the mountains, I had borrowed $10,000 from my parents to help finance my business. I was able to pay them back within six months of working at NetSuite.

However, after about a year and a half, I started feeling restless. The initial excitement began to fade. I had a passion for fitness, and a coach at the gym approached me about participating in bodybuilding competitions. I thought achieving accolades in that area was what I needed, so I decided to enter a fitness show prep that lasted about eight weeks. It was an intense program. I would weigh in with my coach every weekend.

However, there was one thing I couldn't seem to give up. I convinced myself that it wasn't a big deal, especially since I was good at hiding it. I would drink vodka while riding my exercise bike at home. I was dedicated to my diet, eating tilapia and asparagus several times a day, and I was committed to my training, posing, and tanning. But I just couldn't stop drinking.

I also developed a significant dependency on Adderall. I managed to persuade a different psychiatrist that I needed it to "help with focus due to my high-pressure career." I was also prescribed Xanax. Unfortunately, I began abusing both drugs and alcohol, which became my "best friends."

I told myself it wasn't a major issue because I wasn't using cocaine anymore. I felt better about my life because I was showing up for work most days, functioning well enough to get through the week without drinking. However, when happy hour rolled around or when I encountered a nearby bar, I couldn't resist.

Even working fifty to sixty hours a week, I truly enjoyed my work. Finally, I felt I was in an environment set up for success, closing deals, and enjoying the rewards of my efforts. Being able to pay my parents back for that loan and having my first apartment felt like significant accomplishments. Until then, I had gone straight from college to living with two college friends and then with my husband. Though I was nearly twenty-six, this was my first experience living independently.

I thought I was managing well; I was high-functioning, even if I wasn't attending church or addressing underlying issues.

Outside of work, I had some good friends. My drinking habits were becoming more progressive, and after a while, I started feeling unfulfilled at work. I continued bodybuilding and competing; I actually did very well in my competitions. After an eight-week prep, I came in first in my novice class and took third overall, which was a big achievement for me. Still, competing wasn't fulfilling my inner drive.

I wasn't doing cocaine, but I was drinking regularly and searching for opportunities to drink. I continued my familiar pattern of behavior, just in a different context: I had a close girlfriend at work, and we often left during lunch to drink. I would come back absolutely hammered, and since I lived close to bars, it felt normal to me; I also convinced myself it was standard.

Eventually, I got an opportunity to move to Atlanta. A supplement manufacturing company recruited me. They liked my bodybuilding background and my knowledge of selling in the e-commerce space, since this was when people were buying tons of products like fish oil and *Garcinia cambogia* through platforms like Groupon and white-labeling them.

In 2012, I moved to Alpharetta, a suburb of Atlanta. I worked in Norcross for a private-label supplement company and quickly realized there were pills and powders everywhere, along with an open bar in the office. It felt like the Wild West.

Atlanta became a dark time for me. It was the first time I had ever been away from home. My job was 100 percent commission with a draw, and it wasn't what I had expected. I was using drugs regularly, which affected my mood and everything going on in my life. I began traveling frequently for work, flying from Atlanta to Las Vegas or Los Angeles. Partying was a significant part of my job. We often went to strip clubs with clients, many of whom were wealthy, and we were encouraged to socialize with them in various capacities. Thankfully, I still had my two dogs and a roommate who took great care of them during this challenging time.

I often found myself in compromising situations. I would frequently go to downtown Atlanta by myself, enjoying the party atmosphere and sporting events, but I struggled to make or keep friends. I convinced myself that I liked being alone, preferring to drink until the party led me wherever it would. This mentality made it easy for me to avoid explaining my actions to anyone.

However, I ended up in places where I was unwelcome because I was often a drunken mess. I said things I shouldn't have, and to be honest, I don't remember much of that year because I was fairly obliterated for most of it.

On my thirtieth birthday, a friend sent me a birthday package: a Ziploc bag of "Molly." It was some of the purest MDMA[1] crystals I had ever encountered. It was as if cocaine and ecstasy had a baby, and it felt incredible. I remember using it by myself in that house, thinking, *Oh, my gosh, this is amazing!*

I realized I could function well on this substance, remembering things more clearly and experiencing a euphoric high. Soon, I found myself using it before work, before workouts, and even while traveling, without considering the potential consequences. I didn't need to drink as much, but I still would. I felt untouchable.

I was doing okay economically, feeling like I was lucky enough to have my job, yet my way of life was starting to raise red flags. My roommate, now both a confidant of mine and a co-conspirator, was freaked out. I was always late, or I wasn't there at all. At night, we smoked weed together, and I told myself I was only doing it to come down from the Adderall and Molly. It seemed safer than drinking, but it was just another way to manipulate my moods and not make myself feel anything real. I knew something had to give, deep down. These mood swings were starting

---

1. MDMA (short for *3,4-methylenedioxymethamphetamine*) is a synthetic psychoactive drug that affects mood and perception. It's commonly known by street names such as "ecstasy" (in pill form) and "Molly" (in powder or crystal form).

to become extreme, and for some reason, I started feeling burnt out from the semblance of control that I was holding.

A lot of my work took me to Los Angeles and Orange County, and California was always a long, slow breath. My brother and his wife met in a small coastal town where they were married on the sand under the open sky, and it was beautiful. They had a small apartment in San Clemente, splitting their time between California and Denver. Whenever I had shows in L.A. or Anaheim, I would rent a car and drive myself down there, especially if they were out of town. The apartment was directly on the beach, with waves crashing just beyond the window. It was the only place that felt calm to me. I could take a Xanax, crawl into bed, and let the ocean's rhythm drown out the loud noise in my brain. The sound of the waves permitted me to get tired. In that silence, I could almost believe that all was well. It became my sanctuary, a brief escape from the chaos I was too afraid to face.

The pull toward California grew too strong to ignore after I had been working for the supplement company for about a year. I convinced myself that a move would be the solution, that a change of landscape, a new job, and a return to the corporate world would somehow make me whole again.

Self-Reflection: I spent years believing that changing my environment would somehow change me. Every move, every job, every new beginning felt like it might finally fix what was broken inside, but all I ever did was carry the same unhealed pain into a different zip code. I normalized chaos because it matched the storm in my heart. I told myself I was functioning, even thriving, while silently falling apart. The external image I built (the career, the successes, the discipline) became a mask that hid how deeply I was unraveling.

I numbed myself with substances, adrenaline, and constant motion, mistaking survival for strength and escape for freedom. I thought if I stayed busy enough, accomplished enough, or distracted enough, I wouldn't have to face what hurt. I clung to the illusion of control even as my life grew more unmanageable. I kept looking for wholeness in new places, new people, new identities, never realizing that nothing outside of me could heal what I refused to acknowledge within.

In truth, I wasn't running toward a better life; I was running from myself. And every place I landed eventually revealed the same truth that, until I faced my pain, I would repeat my patterns. No new city, no new job, and no new version of me could replace the work that needed to happen on the inside. God wasn't distant. I was. And the very thing I kept trying to outrun was the thing He was calling me to finally face.

Own it: In what ways have you used changes in location, image, or careers to run or hide from pain?

Face it: What emotions or memories keep resurfacing no matter where I go?

Act on it: What's one step I can take today to stop running and start healing (telling one safe person, finding a support community, making an appointment with a therapist, etc.)?

FIVE
CALIFORNIA DREAMIN'

I set out on a quest to find a job at a software company that would allow me to work from home so I could move to the beautiful city of San Clemente. To visualize my goal, I created a vision board and started listening to a song by Hillsong Worship called "Oceans."

Deep down, I felt the need for a significant change in my life, including my habits and extracurricular activities. However, I also held the mistaken belief that simply changing my environment would solve everything.

I interviewed with several software companies, and after a few offers came in, I decided to accept the highest one. This job allowed me to rent an apartment just down the street from my sister-in-law's place, which felt like a dreamy start to my new life. I was ready to begin again.

In July 2013, I packed all my belongings into a pod, took my two dogs, and flew from Atlanta to Los Angeles. My brother was there to pick me up with his kids. On my way to California, I wrote myself a letter about starting fresh. I wanted to keep it as a reminder of my aspirations to live differently.

I envisioned this new chapter as a time to achieve my goals: making a fresh start by moving to California, being the "fun aunt," enjoying Saturday breakfasts with my brother and his kids, going back to church, and getting fit. I felt so resolute about my intentions that I believed I could pass a lie detector test regarding my commitment to change.

Once I arrived, my pod was delivered, and some larger furniture pieces were unloaded. I spent my first night in the new apartment, tempted by the idea of having a bottle of wine, but I reminded myself that I was doing things differently this time.

The next morning, as I began unpacking, a group of cute surfer boys walked by carrying red Solo cups and asked if I was new in town. I said yes, and they invited me to join their barbecue. Before I finished unpacking, I dropped everything and went with them. Within minutes, I had a beer in my hand, and later that night, I ended up at a local bar, where I connected with a drug dealer. It felt like I had a built-in network to find them anywhere. And soon enough, he and I started dating.

Initially, I wasn't looking to get back into anything serious because I had just resolved to lead my life differently. But it quickly became a mix of smoking weed and drinking. I also continued taking Adderall to stay alert and Xanax to help me relax. I felt comfortable in the life I was creating.

Not long after starting my new job, the company took me on a cruise for its annual sales conference, organized by the company that had just moved me from Atlanta and was helping me create my dream life. I asked my psychiatrist to prescribe me medication to prevent any issues, because I did not want to lose this job, and I knew myself well enough to recognize that I could be a hazard to those around me. I needed to make the best impression possible, so I had sought out a prescription drug that, if mixed with alcohol, would make me violently ill. I thought this would serve as my safeguard against drinking on the cruise.

I received the prescription and prepared for the trip. Most of my colleagues were Christians, and I found myself now surrounded by faith-based individuals, which was exciting. They were enthusiastic about having me on board, and it felt like home. I kept telling myself, *Please don't mess this up.*

Despite my intentions, I didn't take the medication. Instead, I convinced myself that this time would be different; I had too much at stake and could manage my drinking. Unfortunately, I didn't manage it well. On the first night, I ended up drunk and crying to one of the wives about my broken relationships and loneliness, definitely not what I had hoped would happen. I struggled with hangovers and showed up to meetings unprepared, far from the capable person I believed I was.

Thankfully, my struggles mainly happened in private, and I worked with compassionate colleagues who were not overly judgmental. However, my pattern continued as I traveled back and forth from California to Sacramento for sales conferences, often drinking excessively during those trips. The work was somewhat monotonous, focused on building their software practice, and it required a self-starter mentality, something that's tough to maintain in a work-from-home environment, especially while dealing with addiction.

I found it difficult to accomplish anything of value or stay motivated. I was sent to trade shows, but my success was limited, even as we were building the business vertically. I loved my job and the incredible people I worked with, and I felt that I was in the right place. Each day, I would wake up determined to do better, telling myself that today would be the day I wouldn't drink. I would plan to take my laptop to a coffee shop to avoid temptation.

Despite my efforts to manage my alcohol consumption, I was also heavily reliant on pills and smoking weed at the time. Balancing all of this became a full-time job. My travels often left me lacking the clarity needed to conduct effective sales meetings.

One day, I received a call from an old colleague from the supplement company where I used to work. His name was "Bill," and he was an older gentleman, a Vietnam vet. We had partied together a lot in the past, and he was an incredible salesman with a charismatic personality. I always referred to him as

"Snaggle Tooth" because, although he was older, he still had a vibrant spirit.

I felt depressed and trapped in my toxic relationship in Park City when he called. He asked how I was doing, and despite my attempts to sound okay, he sensed that I wasn't. Bill was known for his wild partying; he could drink and do drugs like no one else. He always knew how to have a good time.

However, during our conversation, he surprised me by saying he was a year sober. I couldn't believe it. I asked him if it was on purpose, and he confirmed it was. I was astounded. How could he be sober after being such a party guy? He told me he had gone to Alcoholics Anonymous and was ready for a change.

He mentioned that it was important to get to the root causes of why one drinks or uses, and that really struck me. I had never heard anyone say that before. I was genuinely impressed and congratulated him, but I didn't want to share how isolated I felt. Thoughts of suicide had begun to creep in, and I was feeling extremely lonely, although I still had my dogs for companionship.

In September 2015, my brother and his wife had a major issue with me and my consistently irresponsible and reckless behavior. My brother and his wife noticed my behavior and how I interacted with the kids, and he told me he couldn't have me around anymore, which led to a disagreement between his wife and me. They made it clear that I needed to leave; the situation was messy and ugly.

The next day, my brother came to my apartment and told me that I had to change. If I didn't, they didn't want me around for Thanksgiving because he couldn't have me near the kids while I was like this. I actually felt a sense of relief, though I didn't express it to him.

A train ran frequently through our small town at night. As I listened to it, I thought about how, if I didn't have my two dogs, I might throw myself in front of it. Feelings of being a constant disappointment overwhelmed me. I had convinced myself that this situation would last forever.

I even thought about finding a new "mom" for my dogs, someone who would take care of them so I could handle my issues. I went to a dog park I used to frequent, feeling lost and broken, and I was drinking heavily. I let the dogs out of the car, hoping that they might find a new home with someone who loved animals, but no one else was there. I couldn't leave them in an empty park, so I put them back in the car, realizing that this wasn't the plan after all.

Throughout my time in California, I regularly worked out at a group fitness gym called SoCal Boot Camp. I continued to go to workouts, even when I was hungover or high on Adderall. I would be open about my drug use, bragging about how I hadn't slept in three days but was still making it to the gym.

One woman at the bootcamp stood out to me. She had four kids of her own and was adopting two more from Africa. A nurse, she was beautiful and exuded positive energy. Sometimes, we worked together as partners during the workouts. I would brag to her about my wild escapades, feeling like I was living in two very different worlds, and she would often say, "If you ever want to talk about sobriety, I have twenty years of experience."

I always thought that was so strange. I would reply, "Why would I want to talk about sobriety? I'm good. I'm obviously thriving." In reality, I wasn't thriving at all, but I didn't want her to know that.

She would never judge me; instead, she always shared how great her life was. She would laugh at my stories, and she was just so kind and loving. She made me feel like I could be whoever I wanted to be, that I didn't have to hide anything around her.

When my brother said he needed me to make a change and that I shouldn't be around the kids unless I got my act together, she was the first person I thought of. At that time, she was really my only connection (outside of my two dogs) who offered me insight into how I could change.

I wasn't ready to give up my substances entirely, but I was open to trying it for at least 30 days, so I could be invited to the family Thanksgiving without facing any consequences or having to explain myself to my parents.

After my brother's confrontation, he left my apartment, and I reached out to this woman and asked her if she would meet with me because I was struggling. Without hesitation, she agreed to meet that afternoon.

Self-Reflection: Looking back, I can see how hard I tried to outrun myself. Every change of scenery, every new job, and every distraction was just another attempt to escape the parts of me I wasn't ready to face. I kept calling dysfunction "normal" and convincing myself I was fine because I could still perform, produce, and hold it together on the outside. But beneath the surface, I was collapsing. I mistook chaos for excitement, numbness for coping, and high-functioning pain for strength. I didn't realize then that no amount of movement, achievement, or escape could fix what I refused to acknowledge. Healing wasn't waiting for me in a new place; it was waiting for me to stop running.

Own it: Have I ever mistaken fun and freedom for true peace? What "fresh starts" have I convinced myself would fix me?

Face it: No matter where I move or what external circumstances I change, what patterns of behavior keep showing up? How has my attempt to "manage" these feelings actually kept me stuck or in a cycle?

Act on it: Who can I reach out to when I am attempting to escape? What are five other healthy activities I could implement rather than running or trying to escape pain?

SIX
THE GIFT OF AN ESKIMO

On September 9, 2015, I reached out to the person I would later call my "Eskimo," Kathy. An "Eskimo" in the context of Alcoholics Anonymous (AA) refers to someone who introduces you to the recovery process. This person doesn't have to be your sponsor; they simply help you understand that AA is a viable way of life.

She was the only person from my boot camp who I knew was sober and with whom I could be completely honest. We agreed to meet for lunch because I needed help, so we met that afternoon in San Clemente at a little restaurant called Active Culture. I ended up crying my eyes out, and it was the first time in a long while that I could be so honest, despite being at zero days of sobriety.

I told her I felt hopeless, that every day I woke up promising myself that today would be different, only to find myself repeating old patterns by 10 a.m. or noon. I felt trapped in an endless cycle and wanted to die, but I didn't have the courage to take my own life.

Kathy listened intently. Although I didn't talk much about my alcohol use or prescription medications because I wasn't ready to confront those issues, I did express how my family was fed up with me, how I had no meaningful relationships, and that I felt like a shell of a human being who no longer wanted to exist.

After listening, she told me she had good news and bad news. I braced myself and said, "Okay."

She began with the good news: "I felt exactly the way you feel. I went through hopelessness, the desire to change, but being unable to do so on my own. I constantly failed at my resolutions. I want you to know that there's a solution, a way out."

Then she delivered the not-so-good news: "It's Alcoholics Anonymous."

I stared at her, bewildered. AA? "Absolutely not!" I was taken aback. I expected her to prescribe a pill or a powder. Or maybe a retreat. How about a kind of magical solution?

I tried to explain that I didn't understand. I had a job and a degree and a life that wasn't totally wrecked. I didn't drink out of a brown bag. (Of course, that didn't define someone as an alcoholic, but at the time, that was my logic.)

She listened patiently and then said something that would change everything:

"If you keep doing what you're doing, you're going to keep getting what you're getting."

I started to panic as I saw her slide her chair back from the table. I grabbed her wrist, leaned in, and said, "Okay, okay, okay. I'll do anything. I'm that hopeless." So I agreed to try it out for 30 days, and she told me that if I put Alcoholics Anonymous first, above my family, my career, even my relationships and biggest life concerns, those things would begin to fall into place.

"So we must practice it every day," she said. She suggested I begin every morning with an AA meeting. I hesitated. "I can't," I told her. "I work out in the mornings. It would have to be after that."

"Listen," she said firmly. "Put AA first, and everything else will take care of itself."

Oh my goodness, I thought. Okay.

She continued, "There's a clubhouse less than three miles from here. Meetings all day long. But every single day, you're going to have your butt in that 6:30 a.m. meeting. Start your day there."

I walked away from that meeting both terrified and relieved. For the first time in years, I felt understood and sort of hopeful. There was also a sense of strange responsibility, particularly in light of self-outs. She didn't pity or coddle me when I expressed what I felt. She simply said, "Great. Then let's get into a solution right away." Her directness was like oxygen.

That evening, I set my alarm for 6:00 the next morning. Although my ex-husband had sent me to AA before, I hadn't been ready. This time was different. I was genuinely willing, for the first time in my life!

The next morning, my alarm went off. I got up, drove to the meeting, and sat in the parking lot, feeling like my life was over. I couldn't believe I had found myself in this situation, and I was so humiliated and embarrassed. As I walked in, I noticed it was 6:25 a.m., and everyone seemed so happy. The lights felt incredibly bright, and I thought, *What is happening? It's too early for this.*

The topic of the meeting was gratitude, and I thought, *This is so strange.* I sat in the back, and since it was a round-robin format, people went around the room, taking turns sharing their thoughts. In that moment, I found myself judgmental and condescending, thinking I was better than everyone else. I dismissed their experiences at first, thinking, *I bet they didn't even drive themselves here; they probably carpooled, and they likely don't even have home addresses.*

Yet, as I sat there, I started to feel a sense of relief. It was refreshing to be around people who were both happy and sober because, in my experience, those two states never coexisted. I thought I could only be sober and miserable or happy and loaded.

Listening to others share, I heard statements like "I'm grateful to wake up today sober" and "I'm grateful to be in such a beautiful city." Then it hit me: We do live in a paradise.

When it was finally my turn, I could either pass or share. I shared my story. I didn't identify myself as an alcoholic; instead, I introduced myself, saying, "Hi, my name is Kat, and I have a desire to stop drinking." That was the only requirement to attend an AA meeting. I found out later that people even come to AA meetings when they are drunk, as it serves as a supportive environment for alcoholics and addicts.

Although I wasn't ready to accept that I was an alcoholic or believe that I had a problem, I was honest about my desire to stop drinking. By the end, I was crying and pouring my heart out to the room. Cringe.

Kathy had suggested, "Hey, go to as many meetings as you can. If you can't get seven days sober on your own, we really need to consider inpatient rehab." I was taken aback. Inpatient? Rehab? I thought, *No, no, no. I'm not that bad. That's crazy.* But in the back of my mind, I was troubled by the idea of not drinking for seven days. How was I going to do that?

That first day, I went to a noon meeting and later that night visited her house because I didn't trust myself to stay in my apartment without drinking. I didn't experience severe withdrawal like some people describe, but I do remember mornings after when I would wake up shaking from not drinking. I would gag while brushing my teeth, needing a little alcohol in my system just to feel balanced. This was all before I got sober, but I recall "waking up" toward the end of my drinking, realizing it was becoming a problem. There were times I would get up in the middle of the night and drink from a bottle just to calm my nerves. There were definitely mornings when I would shake until I had a drink, and that realization was eye-opening. I realized my body was becoming physically dependent on alcohol, which felt unthinkable.

The discomfort during those first few days was intense. Now that I know more about alcohol and benzodiazepine withdrawals, I realize I might have handled things differently. Alcohol and benzos are the only substances from which you can actually die during withdrawal. During that time, I was still taking a tiny dose of Xanax to help me sleep and had some Adderall on hand. I remember feeling a lot of discomfort, almost crawling out of my skin, but I wanted to change so badly. Kathy believed in me, which kept me motivated to attend meetings morning, noon, and sometimes at night.

When I returned to the meetings, people recognized me and were excited to see me. They would say, "Oh, my gosh, today is your Day Two! We're so excited!" Meanwhile, I thought, *This is awful. Day Two of sobriety? What do you mean? This is terrible.* Secretly, I wasn't planning on staying sober. I was just trying to ease the pressure on my back, hoping they would teach me how to drink like a lady. I imagined being able to open a bottle of wine, cook for friends, and enjoy a nice evening with pasta, salad, and white wine. I had no idea what was ahead of me.

The incredible thing about reaching a point of desperation was that I wanted to change so badly that I was willing to do anything, even if it didn't make sense to me at the time. Kathy advised me to arrive a little early to meetings and help set up. Initially, I was resistant and thought, *Why would I do that?* She explained, "You've been quite selfish and haven't helped anyone in a while. It might be good for you to get out of your head and help others." I finally agreed, thinking, *Okay, that's fine.*

I would arrive a little early and start conversations with people that we couldn't have during the meeting. I really got to know them.

We began talking about our dogs and our interests outside of meetings or work. I learned that some of them had nieces and nephews, too. After the meetings, I would stay to help put the chairs away or clean up, and I found myself making coffee. Before long, people started to know me as the "coffee girl."

It began to feel like a family, and I loved that; I hadn't felt that way in a long time. The differences I initially noticed, such as thinking, *These people aren't like me because they don't have [X, Y, and Z]*, slowly began to fade away. Not only did I feel like I belonged there, but it also felt like a lifeline.

I didn't miss a meeting. They often say to attend "90 meetings in 90 days." For me, it was more like 180 meetings in 90 days, maybe even more, since I was also attending night meetings. I didn't have many friends, so this became a new way of life for me. I finally felt like I was part of something.

At first, I wasn't convinced about the steps or the idea of sponsorship. My ego was still telling me I was better than these people. I thought, *This is cool. I'll just get thirty days and then cruise out of here.* But when my thirty days came, my life started to improve. I felt better about myself, and my workouts at the gym were going well. I decided to stay for another 30 days because I was feeling good.

However, my relationship with my brother and his wife remained strained. When I hit thirty days, nobody threw me a parade; they were proud of me but still cautious. I had done a lot of damage and been very selfish, so they weren't quite ready to fully include me in their lives, and that was understandable.

Self-Reflection: The magic you're looking for is behind the work you're avoiding.

Own it: Where have my ego and pride kept me sick? When have I felt "better than" those who were struggling? What pain have I lived through that uniquely equips me to help others?

Face it: Who in my life is impacted by my negative choices?

Act on it: Who do I know who could be my "Eskimo"? (It could be anyone you know who is currently recovered from addiction/alcoholism whom you could reach out to; proximity is power!)

To get access to resources like AA's 24-hour Zoom meeting or for help with mental illness struggles, scan the QR code for links.

SEVEN
FROM SURVIVAL TO CALLING

Getting sober doesn't fix everything, and I was feeling the full weight of that reality. In those first few months, every emotion I had avoided for years came rushing in at once. I was raw, overwhelmed, and realizing that sobriety didn't erase my problems; it exposed the ones I had buried.

I was sitting in a meeting, bawling my eyes out, completely overwhelmed by emotions I didn't know how to handle. I was about six months sober, but I wasn't working the steps, and I definitely wasn't dealing with any of the underlying issues that kept resurfacing. My sobriety felt fragile, and I felt lost, raw, and disconnected from myself.

The women in the meeting gently encouraged me to get a sponsor, and one of them gave me the number for hers, "Leyla."

When I called her, I could barely get my words out through the tears.

Leyla said, "Wow, I'm honestly shocked that you didn't drink. You are very lucky to still be sober because most people would have picked up by now. We are going to take a very thorough Step One and talk about your powerlessness and how your life is unmanageable. I want you to wait thirty days before you make any decisions."

I was uncomfortable with this approach. I wanted the mess to go away quickly. I wanted to feel better and thought, *Who does she think he is?* I realized I had a "queen" mentality, which is common among alcoholics; I would act like "off with your head" when someone did something wrong, or I would act like a child when I didn't get my way.

I recognized that I had this massive ego combined with an inferiority complex because I didn't have a sense of self. I hadn't worked the steps or addressed the root causes of why I drank and used substances, or why my life felt so unbearable that I wanted to throw myself in front of a train.

This was the first time I had a sponsor, and I was in so much pain that I was willing to take direction. Leyla told me that from then on, I needed to call her every day. She also gave me a list of "Sobriety Sisters," and said I should go to meetings with them. I needed to call at least three of them every single day and start forming friendships with other women.

I was hesitant; I'd always been a tomboy and preferred hanging out with boys. I liked sports and cigars, not typical girl things. My attitude was, I'll call them, but I'm not going to be their friend. Leyla reassured me, saying, "Listen, honey, we all feel that way. Every single girl comes into this program saying she doesn't like women. But guess what? Men are going to pat you on the ass in this program, while the women are going to save your ass."

I started to dial and soon realized that she wasn't wrong. I began to connect with them, and they were cool and just my kind of girls. They were sober, but they still liked to party as much as I did. They thought the same way I did and didn't judge me for the tremendous mistakes I had made. I felt so humiliated, but they were like, "Hey, meet us at this meeting." We would go to dinner afterward, and I didn't feel judged or like an outsider. I truly felt a part of something.

During this time, I started reading the Big Book with my sponsor and really began to see the powerlessness and unmanageability of my situation. I realized it wasn't only about my drinking; it was about my thinking. My thoughts had led me into some terrible circumstances, and if I didn't change how I thought, I would keep making the same ridiculous decisions over and over again.

I went on a quest of self-discovery, focusing on the program, being single, and staying close to my group of women. My sponsor encouraged me to "get in the middle." We went on trips together: camping, to Sedona, and even to a music festival in Boston. For the first time outside of cheerleading, I was experiencing solid friendships with women I could trust. I hadn't trusted myself for a long time, so it was a really cool experience.

I was genuinely working the steps. I wasn't getting high on a relationship, nor was I making insane decisions. My family was encouraging but still seemed skeptical. I was grateful for their support, but wanted to repair our relationship faster. My sponsor kept reminding me, "Keep showing up and doing the right thing. You're not out of the woods yet. We have a long road of reconstruction ahead. You have spent thirty years living a life of self-will, doing whatever you wanted whenever you wanted."

I wanted to take a moment to reflect on that. It was clear to me that regaining the trust I had lost would take time. As I started to work through the steps, I experienced a significant spiritual awakening. I went through the steps relatively quickly because I was in a lot of pain. They often say that the level of pain and desperation you feel typically determines how fast and vigorously you engage with the process, and I certainly felt that urgency. I knew I had to make a change.

One of the coolest experiences I had was celebrating my first year of sobriety. I was shocked that I had managed to reach that milestone, and I was actively sponsoring other women, guiding them through the steps. I was finally in a position to help others. At that time, I was still working at a software company, but I was truly enjoying my sober journey. The relief I felt was incredible; I couldn't believe I had gone an entire year without drugs or alcohol.

When my parents came to visit, it was a completely different experience. There was no awkwardness; I didn't have to hide any bottles or even any complicated relationships. For the first time, I felt free. I had also formed a friendship with my neighbor, who won a plus-one trip to Spain for a sales conference. She invited me to join her, and I thought that sounded amazing, so I went.

I was about fourteen months sober at that point, and while everyone else was attending the conference, I spent the days with the spouses, who were drinking wine and visiting charming little bars. I stuck to sparkling water. We explored many incredible museums during the day, and at night, we hit the nightclubs. I vividly remember dancing in a gay bar until four in the morning, drenched in sweat and feeling exhilarated. I walked out, and it hit me: I just had that experience *sober*. That moment was a revelation for me, a truly spiritual experience.

Spain was so much fun and far more enjoyable than I could have imagined! I realized that I wouldn't have even been invited if I had been drinking, as I probably wouldn't have developed such a meaningful friendship. In the past, I would have been a complete blackout-drunken mess and wouldn't have remembered any of it.

As time went on, I began to embrace this new life, which felt like a world I never knew existed. I wanted everyone to know about this freedom. I started sharing my experiences with friends, emphasizing that you don't have to lose everything to seek help and improve your life. I became passionate about the program, which, to be honest, made my day job feel less exciting. All I wanted to do was attend meetings and work with other women in recovery.

I had a huge vision board in my apartment, and I've always believed in the power of vision boards. I used a whiteboard to create a list and kept a schedule of women I wanted to take beach walks with. During those walks, we would talk and work through various steps, and I'd invite people over for sponsorship meetings. That was a highlight for me. I found myself waking up every day sober in that same apartment where I'd once felt suicidal, and I became obsessed with helping others.

However, as time went on, I started to resent my job because I lost my motivation. When I got sober, I assumed everything would fall into place, that clarity and gratitude alone would allow me to fall in love with my job again. But the opposite happened. The very work I had once used to inflate my ego now seemed meaningless. For years, I had chased titles, commissions, and recognition, but without the chaos and the substances, I couldn't ignore what had always been missing.

I had a clear mind but a divided heart. I would wake up sober and restless every morning. I could no longer pretend that my job made me happy. It held no purpose. Sobriety didn't just remove alcohol; it destroyed the life I had built on the illusion of purpose.

It wasn't that I no longer felt fulfilled by working, but sitting in meetings about sales goals or ERP software evaluations made me feel like a stranger in my own life. Sobriety made that truth impossible to hide. I was beginning to understand that I had not been working toward meaning; I had been working toward survival. Now that I was actually alive, I wanted more than a paycheck. I wanted a purpose.

The tension between who I was becoming and what I was still doing became impossible to ignore. It wasn't burnout. It was awakening.

At that point, I had a few professional mentors whom I had always relied on. When I entered the rooms of Alcoholics Anonymous, I learned a great deal from the women there, but I also gained insight from older gentlemen, most of whom were professionals. I reached out to them for guidance, asking, "Is this normal? I feel like the corporate world might not be for me anymore or that I need a change." They reassured me that it was okay to feel that way, suggesting that while AA wasn't a profession, I should consider making a change if I was truly unhappy.

After some time, I thought about switching companies, but eventually, I decided to take some time off. I realized I could always return to the corporate world later, but I wanted to take the opportunity to figure out what I wanted to do with my life. I was thirty-two at the time, sober for a little over a year and a half, and I decided to leave my company to spend the next few months finding what would bring me fulfillment professionally.

During this time, I had a 401(k), and while working at a supplement company, I had built some valuable relationships that provided me with referral fees. I also had an online skincare side hustle. I've always managed to be self-supporting, but I wanted to focus full-time on discovering my purpose.

I went on a quest, interviewing people I respected professionally and those I saw as having found their purpose. I asked them how they aligned their passion with profit. They consistently told me, "Do what you love, and the money will follow." I realized I loved working with addicts and had a passion for animals, but I knew there wasn't much financial reward in that field. Creating a pet care product didn't appeal to me, so I wrestled with the question: how could I make money while helping addicts? Many people view them as difficult customers because their circumstances often seem chaotic.

One of my mentors suggested, "Why don't you open a rehab?"

I said, "Well, that's crazy because I didn't even go to rehab, so that seems kind of hypocritical."

He replied, "What if you worked in a rehab facility, saw what the experience was like, and were upfront about your intentions? Just see how it goes." I had met a few people in the industry, so I reached out to one of them, and they hired me as a behavioral health care technician for $17 an hour. I worked at a detox residential level of care, assigned to a house right in my town, San Clemente. On my first day, I thought, *Oh, my goodness, I love this!* It was amazing that I could make money doing this while the company was profiting, too. Eventually, it was like a light went on for me: I felt like I could run something like this even better.

You either love working with addicts and alcoholics or you find it overwhelming. The drama can be intense, but for me, it was clear: these are my people, and I understand them. I totally get why someone would throw a fit over not being able to get their nails done when they have only twenty-two hours of sobriety after using gutter water to shoot up heroin. I get it; I'm one of you.

Around this time, I started dating someone I met in Alcoholics Anonymous. He enjoyed helping people like I did, and on our first date, we talked about opening a rehab together. I thought, *Okay, this is kind of cool; we should do this.*

We got serious about opening a rehab. We hired a friend who was familiar with the Treatment Center process to be our consultant. I brought in a hundred grand; my boyfriend (at the time) and business partner contributed another hundred grand from family friends. We basically bootstrapped it together. Our consultant understood our financial limitations and agreed to take some sweat equity to help get us started.

That was in 2017, when I was just under two and a half years sober, and we officially opened our doors at Laguna Shores

Recovery (www.lagunashoresrecovery.com) in October 2018. This marked the beginning of the next chapter in my journey.

Self-Reflection: Sobriety didn't instantly heal me; it revealed me. It exposed the emotions, wounds, and beliefs I had buried under years of distraction, chaos, and survival. In those early months, I realized that the work wasn't just about putting the substances down; it was about surrendering the self-will that had been driving my life into the ground. Every tear, every uncomfortable conversation, every truth I didn't want to face became the soil where God began rebuilding me. I was learning, sometimes painfully, that recovery isn't about controlling my life, it's about letting God remake it.

Own it: What areas of my life are being run on self-will/living on impulse/ignoring what God wants? What do I fear will happen if I truly surrender? Where am I still trying to control outcomes instead of trusting God's plan?

Face it: What emotions have I been trying to outrun that sobriety is now forcing me to finally feel? Where am I still trying to control my life instead of surrendering to God's direction? What patterns, beliefs, or behaviors from my old life are still shaping the way I think today?

Act on it: What's one action I can take to turn this area over, such as asking for accountability and getting a mentor or a spiritual guide to help me walk this out? What step can I take *today* that reflects surrender rather than self-will?

OR

Spend ten minutes today in stillness, asking God (or whatever you believe in) to reveal the next right step, not the *whole* plan, just the next step. Write down what comes up, no matter how small, and take one action toward it within 24 hours.

EIGHT
FROM PAIN TO PURPOSE

The year 2018 was a pivotal one for me. I was thirty-four, and my business partner and I had decided to take a huge leap of faith by going all in and starting our own business, even though we had no idea what we were doing. We knew we loved helping people and wanted to create a stable financial future for ourselves. Working for others had never suited us well, so this was an incredible time of learning.

Let me tell you, opening any kind of business is a journey of self-discovery, but starting a drug and alcohol rehabilitation center brings its own unique challenges and traumas.

We rented a house in Mission Viejo, California, and waited about 6 months for the licensing process to complete, while paying a premium rent of 10 to 20 percent above the usual rate.

While we waited for the state to send us our license, we focused on marketing and branding.

During that time, we also prepared the house by furnishing it and cleaning it up, all while making sure to communicate with the landlord about operating a business at the location. We hired a consultant who sat on our board of directors to help with branding and hiring, while another consultant handled our licensing paperwork.

We networked as much as we could. The wonderful thing about being involved in recovery and opening a treatment center is that everyone within the recovery community wants to help. We had numerous friends who owned or worked at other treatment centers. They were eager to assist us with recommendations for SEO (Search Engine Optimization) services, website developers, billing, and lab services for urinalysis.

In the recovery community, our goal is to be helpful, whether someone is in recovery or not. After spending so much time taking from others and being selfish, we felt it was our time to give back. This experience was truly special. I've owned other businesses in different sectors, like insurance and supplements, but this atmosphere was entirely different, and people often viewed you as competition and guarded their resources closely.

As we were waiting to obtain our official license from the state of California and the Department of Health, I had a memorable experience. My business partner and I flew to Pittsburgh for a sporting event, and while we were away, one of my dogs became seriously ill. These were the dogs I'd had since college, and my Lab, Jackson, was about fifteen years old at the time.

Jackson was aging, but nothing prepared me for the heartache of having to fly home to put him down. It was one of the hardest things I had to face in my sobriety. I still had my Jack Russell, the first dog I ever owned, "Bella," who was around twelve years old at the time. The loss of Jackson was profound and marked a challenging moment in my journey. He was such a good dog. I had never really experienced pain like that during my sobriety.

We had been waiting a long time for our license, and it felt like it was taking forever. The day after we had to put Jackson down, our license finally arrived in the mail, almost like he'd sent it as a gift. We were starting our new business, but I had to say goodbye to my sweet boy, Jackson. It was a bittersweet time.

Despite the pain, I didn't drink. I resumed going to meetings, and I picked up the tools of the program. This was the first real challenge I faced in sobriety. It became a deeply spiritual experience to feel the pain without numbing it.

Not too long after, we booked our first inpatient client. He flew into John Wayne Airport. I took our brand-new minivan to pick him up, and I was so excited to meet him. I felt that excited for all our clients. I couldn't help but hug him and say, "I'm so glad you're here!" It was thrilling to welcome our very first client. I think he was a bit taken aback, especially since he was detoxing. But to this day, that person is still sober! (How cool is that?)

In the first few weeks after we opened, we took in anyone we could. I had a vision that we would run an all-women's or all-men's program, but thank goodness for my business partner. He reminded me that we needed to take whatever clients we could to keep the lights on.

He and I maintained a good balance throughout our partnership. I can be rigid and black-and-white in my thinking, often wanting to help everyone. In contrast, he focused on the business side, what was best for our board and bottom line. I believe that's why we've worked so well together.

We started to see some success. We made plenty of mistakes that no one warns you about; you just have to experience them. Our clients often helped us identify blind spots in our operations and, quite literally, where we needed to "add more cameras." I could fill an entire book with the crazy things I've seen in inpatient detox and rehab settings, but I didn't want that to be our focus. Perhaps another time.

What's really cool is that we began to find success. There's nothing quite like realizing that your business is actually working after jumping in feet first. Other people had faith in us and invested their money, and when it all started to pay off, I felt a sense of belief in myself.

We experienced hard times, but we had an incredible team. The best advice we received was not to splurge on an extravagant house overlooking the ocean. Instead, we were advised to get a modest home and invest in our staff. We focused on hiring amazing people who would feel honored to work with us rather than just putting in hours for a paycheck. Still to this day, we pay our staff 10-20 percent above the industry average and have very low turnover as a result.

Hiring was one of my favorite parts of the process. It's kind of like speed dating in a weird way. I was adamant about wanting to hire everyone with a recovery background. I believe it's challenging for clients to connect with staff who don't have that shared experience, especially when we are essentially selling a lifestyle of recovery.

I do have one employee who isn't in recovery and has proven me wrong. She is amazing. Everyone loves her, and she has been a steady presence in our team. However, she is really the exception to the rule. Everyone has been in recovery for something, it seems. So most of our staff have gone through the same process as our clients.

From the beginning, our goal as a partnership was to hire our clients after they achieved six months of recovery. We aimed to create a community where people feel at home. When clients walked in, we wanted them to think, *Oh, this feels like home.* We decorated and designed our facility to provide the best client experience possible; they are essentially living there for thirty days, and I am the first to tell them this is their home, so please don't hesitate to ask for whatever is needed to feel comfortable. Oftentimes, this includes pets coming in with them or even multiple support animals (which I'm more than okay with).

The fun parts of the business were taking out clients to Costco, having game nights, attending AA, NA (Narcotics Anonymous), or CA (Cocaine Anonymous) meetings, and go to dinner afterward. I wanted to recreate the community I missed so much in my life, and I feel I was able to do that with these clients.

My business partner and I would also take them to activities we enjoyed. We went to places like Six Flags and got floor seats at sporting events, experiences that made us think, *Oh, my gosh, I can't believe I stayed sober through that!*

Eventually, we started to make money, and it was an exciting time for us. We even opened a second house. Then COVID hit, which changed everything in the treatment community. Unlike in recovery, many people stayed home and drank more because they weren't required to work in person. A lot of individuals were drinking around the clock, and there wasn't a strong incentive to get their lives together.

We opened the second house perhaps too soon. After about six months to a year, we temporarily closed it to let things settle down as we awaited clarity about how long the pandemic would last.

When things started to open up again, many people began seeing they had a problem. They hadn't noticed how their drinking had spiraled during the year of isolation, and as they returned to real life and work, they realized, *I need to get my act together.* Interestingly, we saw an influx of clients who didn't fit the typical mold of drug addicts or alcoholics. They were people who had developed a habit of drinking and needed help to stop.

This was encouraging because we started making a profit, which allowed us to buy out our initial investors, including family and friends, as well as a silent investor. Once we had majority shares, we were approached by several individuals who had played significant roles in building other facilities but lacked ownership opportunities. We offered them profit-sharing equity and made them partners, which transformed our business financially.

They came in with a level of professionalism that my partner and I were not quite used to. We had bootstrapped our business together and were genuinely a "mom and pop" operation. We loved spending time with our staff, and I would even be there every holiday.

They approached the idea of recovery from a different perspective, recognizing that not everyone who comes to rehab needs to follow Alcoholics Anonymous. While I had "The Twelve Steps" displayed on the wall and we conducted Big Book groups, they encouraged us to understand that there are various paths to recovery. We had amazing therapists and provided excellent care, but our new business partners pushed us to raise our standards. They suggested improvements like establishing a proper HR department, creating a more professional website, and offering virtual tours. Thanks to their help, our business expanded significantly.

About a year after bringing in additional partners, we added another individual, someone who has been monumental in the industry. We wanted to buy his facility or absorb it, but since he wouldn't sell to us, we instead welcomed him to our team and later opened a mental health facility together.

At the time of my writing, I'm working alongside three new business partners, bringing the total to five, including my existing partner. The professional landscape includes five male business partners and me. Although this situation presents its own challenges, we find ways to make it work. Things are going really well, and we are enjoying the journey. One of the best pieces of advice I received is that knowing who you are doing business with is crucial; your business partners become an intimate part of your life, much like in a marriage. You discuss finances, future plans, passions, and purposes daily, so it's essential to get along. If issues arise, you need a process for resolving them. Just like in any relationship, unresolved disagreements can lead to resentment, which can jeopardize the business.

I feel compelled to share that my original business partner and I were romantically involved during the first four years of our venture. We tried to maintain our romantic relationship while managing the business. While we often seemed polar opposites, we worked well together professionally. Looking back, we had a balanced relationship, and professionally, I can see why God brought us together.

In 2021, after being together and even getting engaged, we decided to go our separate ways. There was no romantic connection; our relationship had become entirely about work, and the business was really the foundation holding us together. Ending the relationship was the best decision we could have made. We weren't meant to be romantic partners, and releasing that allowed us both to move forward in healthier, more aligned ways (though we didn't know it at the time).

This was a challenging decision that raised many questions: What would happen to the business? We had around twenty to twenty-five staff members. What would they think or say? Again, during this tumultuous time, we had wise counsel from our friend and consultant who had originally helped us start our business; he strongly suggested that we make no major decisions and avoid speaking to each other about personal matters for at least 6 months. We needed to allow time for the dust to settle while focusing on the beautiful opportunity we had created, the chance to help people, and build generational wealth. I'm thankful we followed his advice, as it was essential for our business's continuity.

Since then, the company has expanded into three facilities and now includes five additional business partners. While the journey hasn't been perfect, and we have certainly navigated challenges along the way, every experience has ultimately contributed to growth. I am grateful that the partnership continues to function well, that the business is thriving, and that we are able to help so many people. It works for us, even though it is a structure that might not work for everyone.

Self-Reflection: This chapter is a great reminder of what it looks like to act on faith (the promises of the unseen). God has a way of turning pain into purpose, but He can't do that unless we are willing to ACT on it. Imagine if I had decided to shrink back in fear of the unknown or stay in the comfort and "certainty" of corporate America? What would have happened to the hundreds, if not thousands, of people we have been able to help through our programs?

These businesses aren't about me but about the people we employ and the lives we have been able to positively impact through them. And here's the thing... you're never ready. While you're waiting for the perfect partner or perfect season, people are suffering because they need to hear *your* story. That's where faith comes in... I didn't just dream about opening a treatment center. I *acted*! I found a consultant, made a business plan, and signed a lease. Acting on it turned my vision into a reality.

Own it: Where in my life do I need to step out in faith even though I'm not fully ready?

Face it: How might the pain in my life hold a hidden purpose? What fears in my life are holding me back from pursuing God's purpose for me?

Act on it: What is one step of faith I can take *this week* that I have been avoiding that will help me actualize my dreams? What is one meeting I can schedule with someone that I can turn to for guidance or mentorship when it comes to achieving my dream life? What practical action can I take *today* that aligns with getting me *one step* closer to my vision or calling?

NINE
HEALED BY HORSES, HUMBLED BY DOGS

In 2021, I found myself starting over again, standing in the middle of a life that no longer fit and facing the uncertainty of what would come next. I was grieving the version of my life I thought I wanted and trying to figure out who I was becoming. Everything felt unfamiliar, and I was searching for something steady, something grounding.

During that time, I started spending a lot of afternoons down at the horse stables. A girlfriend from my recovery group, whom I'd met back when we were both working at a treatment center for $17 an hour, invited me to come visit the stables in San Juan Capistrano. I've always had a strong affinity for horses; being around them felt like a return to something true and familiar. All of my childhood artwork that my parents saved has horses everywhere. I used to ride as a little girl, thanks to riding lessons from one of my mom's high school students. I was still obsessed with horses.

Horses are natural healers. Most people don't realize that they possess acute instincts because they lack sharp claws or teeth for defense. As a survival mechanism, they are very aware of their surroundings. Remarkably, they can feel your heartbeat from almost a hundred yards away, and if you're next to a horse, they can synchronize their heartbeat with yours within about ninety seconds. If they sense that your heart is racing, they'll slow down their heartbeat to help calm you.

Many people don't understand this, but it's one of the reasons we use horses for therapeutic purposes: they have an incredible healing energy. They can also act as a mirror; if they sense turmoil in you, they might not come near. This means you need to stay calm while being around them.

I immediately fell in love with the horse stables and the incredible animals there. It became a sanctuary where I could escape my problems and separate from the Alcoholics Anonymous meetings I attended.

Around the same time, another woman from my program contacted me and asked if I would like to foster a puppy. I was surprised and asked her what she meant by fostering. She explained that she worked with an organization called Doggie Bonez (Home - Doggie Bonez Dog & Puppy Rescue), which rescues dogs that are homeless or at risk of euthanasia. It is entirely foster-based, as they don't have a physical facility, so they need people like us to care for the dogs while they get ready for adoption. I thought that sounded amazing and agreed to participate. My first foster was a little Rottweiler puppy.

At that time, I still had Bella, my Jack Russell Terrier, and I adopted a long-haired Chihuahua, Winston, a year or so after I put Jackson down. Winston was a peculiar case; he had been saved from a kill shelter in L.A. before coming to live with us. He hated everyone and wouldn't even come out for a walk at the pound. When we put the leash on him, he curled up on the floor, and the staff had to drag him out. Despite my reservations and believing that adopting a dog with such a fearful demeanor was a terrible idea, I couldn't leave this little guy, so I brought him home. Fortunately, he and my Jack Russell Terrier get along great.

When I brought home this new little Rottweiler puppy to foster, he was not welcomed by my two smaller dogs. But I was obsessed with him; I took him everywhere. I thought, *This is the coolest thing ever!* I'd always wanted lots of dogs, and I started bringing the puppy to the rehab center. (I mean, who doesn't love puppies, right?) They immediately brought everyone together.

Then the puppy got adopted, and I was shocked, thinking, *Wait, what do you mean he already found a home?* I bawled my eyes out. I couldn't believe it. The person at the agency said, "But I have this other puppy," and she just gave me another one, even though I didn't want a different dog.

This experience was a real learning opportunity because I love dogs so much. I know these animals would have been put down if it weren't for me. They need a foster home, but the downside is that they aren't mine, and I get attached very easily.

This theme of purpose over pleasure has been prominent in my life. One of my purposes is to help people and animals, but I can't keep helping animals if I keep them, so I have to remind myself of that every day.

I also got pretty involved with Doggie Bonez, doing weekend adoption events where all the fosters showcased their dogs. An amazing benefit of this was that I sometimes took multiple dogs or puppies to my rehab facilities. Clients loved it; after all, who wouldn't enjoy puppies when they come into rehab feeling broken, sad, or sick?

One of my goals in creating my facilities was to make them animal-friendly. A major reason I was hesitant to admit myself into a facility was that I had my two dogs, but no one to take care of them. So, we allow clients to bring their animals to our facilities, assuming their pets are up to date on vaccinations and are friendly with both animals and people. We welcome everyone just as they are. (And honestly, we sometimes like the animals more than the people!)

This was a great time, and my staff loved it too. I ended up fostering an entire litter of German Shepherd-Pitbull puppies, some of which my staff adopted. It was wonderful, as I still get to see them.

There's nothing cooler than having a backseat full of puppies while driving to my rehabs and spreading joy and happiness. Dog fostering has taught me a lot about myself. I've also learned detachment. Some friends tell me I'm not cut out for dog fostering because I cry when they leave. I even buy them collars, name them, and get their DNA tested, just in case I want to keep them. It can feel overwhelming at times. I constantly have to remind myself that these dogs are not mine; they are on loan. When they find a home, my job is done.

One of the coolest cases involved a little Chihuahua I rescued from Tijuana. When we found him, he was tied up to a tree. We pulled him to safety, but he was completely emaciated and didn't trust people at all. He was angry, scared, and sad.

One night, they dropped him off at my house, and he wouldn't even come near me. When I opened his crate, he ran outside. To help him feel secure, I placed his crate by the back patio door so he could sleep in it. He still wouldn't get close to anyone.

Humans had been very cruel to him. Every night, I moved his crate a little closer to my bedroom. I started from outside, then brought it inside the patio door, then to the kitchen, and finally to just outside my bedroom door. Within four or five days, he was sleeping right outside my bedroom when I woke up.

He no longer ran outside, though he still wouldn't let me pick him up. At least he was letting me get close to him and feed him.

He was such a cool dog, and I had him for about three weeks. My other dogs actually welcomed him, and he became a little buddy to them. Now he has a loving home. I worked hard with him because he wasn't one I could bring to my facilities right away. Socializing him was crucial; there was no chance he would have gotten adopted if he had gone straight into a shelter. He needed to learn to trust humans again, and that took a lot of work, but it was so rewarding.

I still receive pictures from the people who successfully adopted him. To me, my dogs are like my kids, so it's an incredible honor to be part of that process. Many animals wouldn't have been adopted in the state they were in when they were dropped off.

By socializing them, especially those with less anxiety who just need love, I can take them to my facilities. It's a win-win situation: my clients get to love them, and they get to feel loved and socialized. After a while, they are easily adopted because they have developed their personalities, confidence, and sense of safety. This is one of my favorite things in the world.

Healing doesn't always happen in hospitals or therapy rooms. Sometimes it's found in a stable, a dog rescue, or in the quiet act of caring for something more vulnerable than you. The same love that mends others is the love that restores you.

Self-Reflection: Starting over showed me that healing doesn't always look like progress on paper; sometimes it looks like standing still long enough to let God redirect you. In a season where I felt unanchored, the stables and the rescue dogs became places where I could breathe again. The horses mirrored my internal state, forcing me to slow down, soften, and feel. The dogs reminded me what trust looks like when it's rebuilt slowly and patiently. Caring for these animals grounded me in a way that meetings, work, and structure couldn't. It humbled me, softened me, and reminded me that purpose often finds you while you're helping something unable to help itself. In tending to them, I was unknowingly tending to the parts of myself that still needed patience, gentleness, and grace.

Own it: What in my life is God using to heal me that I keep overlooking because it doesn't look like "purpose"?

Face it: What would it look like to trust that purpose doesn't have to be forced or found but *revealed* through daily acts of service, presence, and compassion?

Act on it: Spend time this week serving something outside of yourself, walk shelter dogs, volunteer, check on a friend in recovery, or care for an animal or person who needs love. As you serve, ask: *What is this teaching me about who I'm becoming?* Then, journal one paragraph each night on how giving heals the giver.

TEN
THE RISE OF SOBERKATT: OWNING MY STORY OUT LOUD

In 2021 and 2022, I really started getting serious about going back to the gym and investing time in myself. I also felt it was the right moment to share my story on social media and recover "out loud." That's when I began posting about my recovery journey and my lifestyle.

Initially, my page was called SocalKatt, short for Southern California Kat, but I later changed it to SoberKatt. It was an exciting time because my businesses were thriving and no longer required my constant involvement. So, I thought, *What can I do next?* I started focusing on building my personal brand, being a voice for those struggling in silence.

I began doing podcasts and speaking on stages, reaching a point where I wasn't embarrassed about being in recovery and felt proud about turning my pain into purpose.

I created my online platform through Instagram and became more courageous about sharing what it was like to be a "high-functioning" addict/alcoholic. I started traveling and demonstrating that it's possible to visit places like Colombia and remain sober, even during extravagant trips where champagne is flowing. I really found my comfort zone in sharing my personal brand.

Self-Reflection: It's evident that I move at the speed of pain. Relationship pain forced me to seek emotional healing again, this time not in another romantic relationship but through service to animals in need and other humans. I had no idea that God would give me so much fulfillment in being "out of self." Formula for happiness: less of me, more of *you*!

Own it: How have I been relying on distractions instead of leaning in to healing? Where is the first place I go when I feel hurt, neglected, or rejected? What are my natural affinities (such as a love for animals) that I've neglected that could actually help me heal?

Face it: Where have I been using momentum, productivity, posting, or building as a way to avoid sitting with my pain? What parts of my story have I been too afraid or ashamed to share, even though they could set someone else free?

Act on it: What small act of service or care for someone/something else can I do *today* to get out of self? Who could I reach out to this week to help me turn my pain into purpose? What rituals or routines (like visiting the stables or volunteering with a local rescue) would be helpful for me to process my feelings constructively?

ELEVEN
THE QUEENS CALL

It all happened almost simultaneously, and looking back, it still feels surreal. One morning in January 2024, during my quiet time with God, I felt an unexpected nudge. A single mom on our billing team had been on my mind, and I felt God clearly tell me to bless her with a massage at the Montage. It made no sense to me. I had never been to the Montage before, and I lived just ten minutes from the Ritz-Carlton. Naturally, I thought, *Why not just go to the Ritz?* But the prompting persisted, loud, repetitive, insistent. So I went.

I drove to Laguna, parked, and wandered around until I found the spa. On my way, I passed a whiteboard that said "The Queen's Table." Something about it caught my attention. (I even took a video before a hotel attendant politely shooed me away.) I bought the massage and left, confused but obedient. I had no idea that this small act of obedience was the beginning of an entirely new chapter of purpose.

A few weeks later, I was invited to a women's church retreat in Idaho. I didn't want to go. The friend who invited me bailed last minute, and on my way to the airport, I nearly turned around. But again, I felt that quiet insistence from God: *Go.* And so I went. When I arrived, two women from the church picked me up. To my surprise, they were incredible, professional, single, health-focused, passionate about Jesus… women I instantly felt drawn to. I remember thinking, *Wow. I need more friendships like this.*

They introduced me to Live Out Loud, a faith-based network led by Brooke Thomas. One of them casually mentioned that the real ballers sometimes get invited to something called The Queen's Table. When she explained that it was an exclusive group of high-level entrepreneurial women: millionaires and billionaires who combine business with Kingdom impact, something clicked. Then I showed her the video from the Montage. Her face lit up. "Kat, that was their retreat."

Everything inside me froze for a moment. God had walked me straight into a place I didn't even know existed.

That night, she added me to a group thread with Brooke. We spoke briefly, and I told her that I didn't fully understand what The Queen's Table was, but I felt drawn to it. She told me they rarely let in new members mid-year, but after hearing my story, she felt led to bring it to the group. When I got back from

Idaho, she and I met in Newport. Listening to her talk about her marriage, her business, and the mission of her community regarding profit with purpose and women building for God's Kingdom, I knew instantly: **This is where I'm supposed to be.**

I was able to join The Queen's Table shortly after. Sitting at that table for the first time, surrounded by women who had built empires and were using their resources to create real impact, something inside me expanded. Before I joined, they had raised half a million dollars in a single week to build a safe house in Greece for victims of sex trafficking. Now that safe house stands as proof of what happens when women of faith combine purpose with power. These women weren't just successful; they were surrendered. They were generous, strategic, bold, and always asking, *How can we help?*

Being part of this group reshaped me. It elevated my thinking, deepened my faith, and taught me how to integrate God into every part of my business without hesitation or apology. These women became my sisters, my "iron-sharpening-iron," teaching me what it looks like to build not just a business, but a legacy for God's Kingdom.

They also played a major role in the creation of my free online sobriety community, Chains to Changed. By late 2024, my inbox was overflowing with people secretly asking for help with sobriety. They were ashamed, hiding, terrified to walk into an AA meeting, and longing for a place to feel seen. I kept hearing the same whisper from God: *Build it. If not you, then who?*

I resisted at first. Building a community takes time, money, and emotional bandwidth, but the nudge wouldn't leave. And I've learned that the things I resist the most are usually the things God needs me to step into. So I built it. Chains to Changed became a 24/7, anonymous, global sober community offering meetings, resources, sober lifestyle ideas, and most importantly, accountability. I created a Sobriety Journal to go with it: daily goals, gratitude, faith, structure, and the heart of the community became the Daily Non-Negotiables, where members check in morning and night.

In less than a year, we grew to over 1,060 members. People found their footing, their hope, their people. They created sober lives they didn't want to escape from. I read their wins every day:

"First college football game sober."

"My daughter saw me sober all weekend."

"My marriage is healing."

"I've lost fifteen pounds and love sober gym life."

God took a whisper and turned it into a global movement.

Looking back, I can see so clearly that every nudge, every discomfort, every obedience led me to exactly where I needed to be. God put me in rooms I didn't feel qualified for but that I was called to. He connected me to women who expanded my faith and my future. And He took my surrender and used it to reach people around the world.

I still don't know where God is taking C2C or The Queen's Table or even the fullness of my calling, but I know this: when God whispers, you go. Every blessing on the other side has been worth the risk.

Self-Reflection: Looking back, I can see that God was orchestrating every detail long before I understood what He was doing. The small, inconvenient nudges, the Montage, Idaho, the women I met, and the conversations I didn't expect were all stepping stones into the next version of my calling. Obedience didn't always feel comfortable, but it always produced clarity. Every time I said yes, another door opened. Every time I showed up, God showed me what was possible.

I am realizing now that purpose isn't found in striving; it is found in responding. It is found in the moments where faith overrides logic, comfort, or convenience. God didn't just guide me into new rooms; He used those rooms to reveal who I was becoming.

Own it: I've spent a lot of time trying to control my own path, forgetting that obedience, not strategy, creates the biggest breakthroughs. I've avoided certain people, rooms, or opportunities because I didn't think I belonged there.

Face it: Where am I resisting God's direction because it feels inconvenient, unfamiliar, or uncomfortable? Where do I default to self-reliance instead of surrender? What doors might already be opening around me that I'm too distracted or fearful to recognize? Where is God calling me higher, even if I don't feel ready?

Act on it: What small act of obedience can I take today, even if it doesn't make sense yet? Who is God prompting me to reach out to, invest in, or learn from? What community, conversation, or room do I need to step into, even if I'm nervous? What leap of faith can I take this week that aligns with the woman I'm becoming, not the woman I've been?

TWELVE
DISCIPLINE, ALIGNMENT & THE GYM THAT CHANGED EVERYTHING

Additionally, in 2024, I was introduced to a new gym. It might sound silly, but gyms have always been a grounding place for me. I'd had personal trainers before, but a friend insisted I try this one. *"Yes, it's thirty minutes away, but I promise you it's worth it."*

When I arrived in Oceanside, I immediately felt at home. The vibe was nothing like the polished health clubs where people spent more time scrolling on their phones or heading downstairs for Botox. This was a real bodybuilding gym. Loud music. No air conditioning. Machines I had never seen before. Every person in the room looked like discipline carved into human form. I walked in thinking, *I want what everyone here has.*

At my old gym, I felt like the top dog, but there's a danger in being the most accomplished person in the room; you stop growing. Here, I was the beginner again in the best way. So I started making the thirty-minute drive every day.

I began training with the owner, a first-generation immigrant from Poland who built everything from nothing. He grew up poor, served in the military, bought his home with a VA loan, and eventually invested in the gym. By the time I met him, he had won Mr. California, owned multiple properties, and drove a Lamborghini, not because life was handed to him but because he refused to let comfort dictate his future.

His coaching style was exactly what I needed. He pushed me physically, but more importantly, he pushed the part of me that still wanted comfort. He reminded me daily that discomfort is the doorway to transformation.

And as much as people don't like to admit it, being fit changes the way the world treats you. The truth? People trust discipline. They trust someone who clearly takes ownership of their life. I'm not saying it's fair, I'm saying it's real. And I leaned into it.

Through this process, my self-confidence transformed. I began building a physique I was genuinely proud of, but even more powerful was the identity shift happening underneath.

My coach handled my nutrition plan, and a chef handled the prep, but *I* handled the execution. Not a single thing went into my body without intention. And as the physical changes came, I realized:

If I can push through cravings, exhaustion, the cold plunge at 39 degrees every morning, and the desire to quit on leg day... I can push through anything God calls me to.

The gym wasn't about aesthetics; it was a daily reminder that discipline creates freedom. Consistency creates confidence. Habits create destiny.

People started to comment on my transformation, but what they really saw was the result of thousands of quiet decisions no one applauded: reading my Bible every morning, cold plunging, showing up to the gym exhausted, drinking a gallon and a half of water, going to bed early, fueling my body with precision, and aligning my day with my purpose.

These became my Daily Non-Negotiables, the same habits I now teach inside the Chains to Changed Academy for women who want to go from sober... to stable... to unstoppable.

Sobriety cleared the fog, but discipline built the foundation. It wasn't enough to simply not drink. I wanted to build a life that honored the calling God placed on me. How could I expect to lead others if I wasn't leading myself?

And let me say this clearly: Most people think the transformation is physical. It's not. It's spiritual. Because if I don't feed my spirit first, I will start reaching for things that can't fix anything. That connection with God has become my anchor. Without it, discipline collapses into self-reliance. With it, discipline becomes worship.

My days now follow a rhythm that supports who I'm becoming:

- Time with God every morning (6 a.m.)
- Journal and *write* every single one of my goals + daily action plan
- Cold plunge
- Gym and/or 10,000 steps
- Meal prep
- Hydration (at least 1 Gal of water)
- AA meeting or helping another alcoholic
- Nightly review (Did I meet my goals today? How can I make tomorrow better?)
- Early bedtime (9 p.m.)

It sounds like a lot, and sometimes it feels like a lot. But I wake up every day with a clean slate. I stack my wins one by one. I show up even when I don't feel like it. I choose alignment over emotion.

People ask me about motivation, and I tell them the truth: I'm not motivated. I'm disciplined. Motivation is a feeling. Discipline is a decision.

And that decision has transformed every area of my life. If I ever find myself being the most accomplished person in the room, I leave. Because growth only happens around people who stretch you. The gym gave me that. AA gave me that. My mentors gave me that. God gave me that. Discipline didn't just build my body, it built my character.

Self-Reflection: The more time I spend in God's Word and actually *acting* on the nudges He gives me, the clearer His voice becomes. Alignment, discipline, and community have been the engines of my growth over the past eighteen months. When I stopped doing things my way and surrounded myself with people who embodied excellence, my entire life was elevated with them.

I am running a few minutes late; my previous meeting is running over.

Own it: I acknowledge that the life I want requires habits I've been avoiding. I acknowledge that discipline is a spiritual practice, not punishment. I acknowledge that God nudges me more often than I admit, and I've been ignoring Him.
I acknowledge that excellence is my responsibility, not luck.
I acknowledge that consistency, not intensity, is what will change my life.

Face it: Where am I still choosing comfort over calling? Where am I hoping for change while avoiding the habits that create it? Where am I shrinking my standards to match my feelings? Where am I refusing the environments that would stretch me? Where am I spiritually undernourished and expecting physical solutions to fix it?

Act on it: What is one physical habit I can commit to daily without negotiation? What is one spiritual habit I will prioritize before anything else? What community could I join that would elevate me? What investment in myself have I delayed that I know is necessary?

CONCLUSION

On my journey from identity struggles to addiction to finding my faith and turning pain into purpose, there has been one undeniable truth: God's plan is *always* bigger than our own. I would have sold myself short if I'd settled for the life I'd dreamed of, with corporate success and business suits. Who knew a life of purpose, fulfillment, and usefulness was on the other side of my surrender?

I want you to know that *your* story matters. Your struggles, your victories, the darkest, most shameful moments in your past are actually God's tools to light the path for someone else. People are suffering in the dark who need to hear *your* story, not mine, not your brothers or sisters, but *yours*.

As you close this book, I want you to ask yourself: *What mountain has God placed in front of me to climb and show others the way?* It's time to rise, lead, and inspire. The journey is not easy, and you will probably stumble, as we all do, but every step you take is a small victory that will add up to a life of impact.

Your story is someone else's survival guide! What are you waiting for?

P.S. Here are a few beautiful updates since I first began writing this book…

Over the past year, God has rewritten parts of my story I didn't even know were missing. I met the man of my dreams, and we'll be married by the end of 2025. He is more than everything I prayed for: a man who leads with faith, walks in purpose, loves deeply, and partners with me in the mission of helping others heal.

In November, I celebrated ten years sober. A full decade. A miracle that still brings me to my knees in gratitude. I also became a best-selling author after co-authoring She Nailed It, a milestone that reminded me how powerful our stories can be when we share them boldly.

On the business side, we bought out two of our partners, bringing our leadership down to four. Our commitment remains the same: to bring light into dark places and help people rebuild their lives with dignity and hope.

And one of my greatest joys this year has been launching my coaching platform for high-performing sober women who feel sober but stuck, and who are ready to transform their identity, build structure, find purpose, and actually thrive in the life they once prayed for.

God is moving.

The story is unfolding.

And this book is part of that journey.

THANK YOU FOR READING MY BOOK!

You can find links to everything mentioned: programs, coaching, community, and resources by scanning the QR code below.

I appreciate your interest in my book and value your feedback, as it helps me improve future versions. I would appreciate it if you could leave your invaluable review on Amazon.com with your feedback. Thank you!

www.ingramcontent.com/pod-product-compliance
Lightning Source LLC
LaVergne TN
LVHW051842080426
835512LV00018B/3026